The Expert Le

The Expert Learner

Challenging the Myth of Ability

Gordon Stobart

 Open University Press

Open University Press
McGraw-Hill Education
McGraw-Hill House
Shoppenhangers Road
Maidenhead
Berkshire
England
SL6 2QL

email: enquiries@openup.co.uk
world wide web: www.openup.co.uk

and Two Penn Plaza, New York, NY 10121-2289, USA

First published 2014

A catalogue record of this book is available from the British Library

ISBN-13: 978-0-33-524730-1 (pb)
ISBN-10: 0-33-524730-X (pb)
eISBN: 978-0-33-524731-8

Library of Congress Cataloging-in-Publication Data
CIP data applied for

Typesetting and e-book compilations by
RefineCatch Limited, Bungay, Suffolk

Printed and bound by CPI Group (UK) Ltd, Croydon, CR0 4YY

Praise for this book

"Highly readable, plenty of examples, and packed with the power of thinking about learning in a way that can make the difference.

This is a book full of optimism – it offers a way to positively think about learning and schools. We are not determined by birth, social status, poverty, wealth ... but we can invest in our learning if we 'think' appropriately. Stobart emphasizes not just practice, but deliberate coached practice, he shows the multiplier effect that comes from seizing opportunities or someone creating opportunities, and he shows the importance of risk taking, deep knowledge, creativity, and developing talk about progress."

John Hattie, Director, Melbourne Education Research Institute,
University of Melbourne, Australia

"If I were to recommend just one book that all teachers, parents, employers and politicians who are interested in education should read, it would be this one. Not only is it full of engaging stories, underpinned by important research, but it goes to the very heart of what it is to be a successful learner and effective teacher It demolishes the myth of inherited ability as the overriding determinant of achievement and provides an alternative account by unpacking the opportunities, experiences and practices that lead to the development of true expertise. Read it and use the ideas to challenge backward thinking."

Professor Mary James, University of Cambridge, UK

"With clear arguments and ample research evidence, Stobart dispels the myth of ability and shows us the harm of society's persistent reliance on repackaged IQ tests. He advocates, instead, for teaching methods and schools that open up rather than close down opportunities. Using research on expertise and compelling examples from sports, science, medicine, and music, this book shows us how good teaching practices -- such as rich questioning and supportive feedback – can engage students in the kinds of deep and purposeful practice needed for adept, expert learning. All students can benefit from this model of teaching, not just an elite few."

Distinguished Professor Lorrie Shepard,
University of Colorado Boulder, USA

Contents

CONTENTS

Series Editors' Introduction

Expanding Educational Horizons

In confronting the many challenges that the future holds in store, humankind sees in education an indispensable asset . . .

(Delors et al., 1996)[4]

The dizzying speed of the modern world puts education at the heart of both personal and community development; its mission is to enable everyone, without exception, to develop all their talents to the full and to realize their creative potential, including responsibility for their own lives and achievement of their personal aims.

Education, unfortunately, doesn't always keep up with the times. Sometimes it appears to be moving in step with changes; at other times it still seems to be in the past century. Many years of research have shown us that tinkering around the edges of schooling won't help educators meet the challenges that children and young people will face in their future. Current interventions are having limited effects.[2] Even if levels of attainment are getting better, the gap in educational achievement between the most and least advantaged is far too wide in many places. Every child and young person has to be well equipped to seize learning opportunities throughout life, to broaden her or his knowledge, skills and attitudes, and to be able to adapt to a changing, complex and interconnected world.[3] It's possible to maximize the opportunity of achieving 'preferred futures' for children and young people,[1] for the teaching profession, and for schools. But what's required is a bold and imaginative reorientation to educational purposes, policies and practices.

In this series, we want to provide a forum for suggesting and thinking about different and more powerful ways of ensuring that all students are prepared to take an active and proactive role in their future, that all teachers and other adults are best able to help them learn effectively, that all leaders and community members can rise to the challenges of ensuring that nothing stands in their way, and that learning environments are designed in such a way to ensure this high-level learning and success for all students. We believe it's time to expand educational horizons.

Authors in this international series provide fresh views on things we take for granted and alternative ways of addressing educational challenges. Exploring trends, ideas, current and emerging developments and professional learning needs, they offer a variety of perspectives of what education could be; not what it has been or, even, is. The books are designed to engage your imagination, to inform, to encourage you to 'look beyond' and help others to do so, to challenge thinking, to inspire, to motivate, to promote deep reflection, collaboration and thoughtful action, to stimulate learning and deep change; and to offer avenues of action and concrete possibilities.

We hope that the series will appeal to a wide audience of practitioners, local authority/district personnel, professional developers, policy-makers and applied academics working in a variety of different contexts and countries. Primarily, we are looking to support and challenge busy professionals working in education who don't always feel they have time to read books. The research on professional learning that makes a difference is clear: educators need the stimulus of external ideas.[4] The books are intended for use by people in schools/centres/colleges, local authorities/districts, consultants; national, state and regional policy-makers; and professional developers, for example, those involved in leadership development. They will be valuable for people involved in ongoing professional learning programmes. They may also be important additions to Master's courses that are geared to investigating practice as it is and as it might be.

The books are deliberately relatively short, laid out in a way that we hope will add to readability, and contain practical suggestions for action, questions for discussion and to stimulate learning conversations, highlighted quotes and suggested follow-up readings. Each book can be read as a stand-alone text, but the focus on looking beyond what is to what might be is the linking feature, and each book has a broadly similar format, to facilitate the connections.

In this book, *The Expert Learner*, Gordon Stobart takes us on a guided tour of expertise in the worlds of sport, music, science, medicine and even firefighting as he challenges educators to look at what is known about top performers and apply knowledge of how they learn to everyday teaching and learning. Questioning the myth of ability, he shows us how findings about expertise are, in his words, 'far more ordinary than the mysterious processes of the "natural talent" approach' (p.3). The book explores hallmarks of expertise in relation to expectations and goals, mental frameworks and diagnostic decisions of teachers, and argues that expert learners and teachers are more likely to be found in expert schools that invest time in the deliberate practice of the skills of teaching and leadership. It makes sense to us.

Louise Stoll and Lorna Earl

References

1 Beare, H. (2001) *Creating the Future School.* London: RoutledgeFalmer.
2 Coburn, C. (2003) Rethinking scale: moving beyond numbers to deep and lasting change, *Educational Researcher,* 32(6): 3–12.
   Elmore, R. (2004) *School Reform from the Inside Out: Policy, Practice and Performance.* Cambridge, MA: Harvard Education Press.
3 Delors, J., Al Mufti, I., Amagi, A., Carneiro, R., Chung, F., Geremek, B., Gorham, W., Kornhauser, A., Manley, M., Padrón Quero, M., Savané, M-A., Singh, K., Stavenhagen, R., Suhr, M. W. and Nanzhao, Z. (1996) *Learning: The Treasure Within – Report to UNESCO of the International Commission on Education for the Twenty-first Century.* Paris: UNESCO.
4 Cordingley, P., Bell, M., Isham, C., Evans, D. and Firth, A. (2007) What do specialists do in CPD programmes for which there is evidence of positive outcomes for pupils and teachers? Report in *Research Evidence in Education Library.* London: EPPI-Centre, Social Science Research Unit, Institute of Education, University of London.
   Timperley, H., Wilson, A., Barrar, H. and Fung, I. (2008) *Teacher Professional Learning and Development: Best Evidence Synthesis Iteration.* Wellington, New Zealand: Ministry of Education.

Acknowledgements

The spark for this book came from reading, and being excited by, Malcolm Gladwell's best-selling *Outliers: The Story of Success*. This led me to other books, in particular Matthew Syed's *Bounce: How Champions Are Made* and David Shenk's *The Genius in All of Us*. Each of these investigates what lies behind top performance – be it in music, sport, business or science and challenges current 'talent myths'.

As I explored this theme in the academic literature on expertise and expert performance, an area in which the American Anders Ericsson has been pre-eminent for over thirty years, I was struck by how little impact the findings have had on education and how little educational research has contributed to them.

This book seeks to redress this neglect. My thanks go to the series' editors, Louise Stoll and Lorna Earl, for their immediate enthusiasm for this project and their work on improving the initial drafts. I am also grateful to friends and colleagues who have encouraged me and offered valuable ideas, particularly Jo-Anne Baird, Laura Jenner, Steve Edwards and Andrew Macalpine. Special thanks go to my wife Marie Adams for her continuous support and encouragement throughout the daunting process of moving from an idea to a book.

Introduction

Question: What do Wolfgang Amadeus Mozart and David Robert Joseph Beckham have in common?
Answer: Much more than we may think.

At their peak both can be seen as sublime performers in their respective fields. The popular image of Mozart is of a child musical genius who at a relatively young age composed music that has moved audiences for over 100 years. For Beckham, a name and face recognized across the world, it is about 'Bend it like Beckham' free kicks and pinpoint 60-yard passes.

But the similarities go much deeper than 'both were brilliant at what they did'. What was it that enabled both of them to reach this level of expertise? This book tries to answer this question for those such as Beckham and Mozart and the many experts at the top of their fields. It then applies the answers to the everyday world of teaching and learning. The intention is not to turn out lots of little Beckhams and Mozarts, though it would be good to have a few, but to produce students[1] who know how to learn effectively and how to think for themselves in the subjects they

1

study – 'knowing what to do when you don't know what to do'.[2] Expertise results from developing and deliberately practising such skills in a particular domain that, as we shall see, depends on opportunities, motivation, practice and support.

I am not taking the easy way out and putting the success of Mozart and Beckham down to some inborn ability, natural aptitude or genetic good fortune. This is simplistic thinking, along the lines of immediately declaring something 'miraculous', for example, the human eye, thus ending the search for what makes it so complex and wonderful. Top performers are ordinary members of the human race who have developed exceptional skills rather than a group whose God-given (or gene-given) endowments separate them at birth from the rest of us.

So what has happened that makes top performers able to do things the rest of us can only stand back and admire? This is a question that has led researchers to systematically study expert performance. These studies range across music, sport, chess and occupational expertise in such areas as medicine and business.[3] The findings have been popularized in best-sellers such as Malcolm Gladwell's *Outliers*[4] and Matthew Syed's *Bounce*.[5]

I define *expert learning* as the mastery of skills and knowledge at a level that distinguishes the expert from others. Experts, especially in relation to novices, are likely to excel in:

- choosing the appropriate strategy to use;
- generating the best solution, often faster and more accurately than others;
- using superior detection and recognition, for example, seeing patterns and 'deep structures' of a problem;
- applying extensive qualitative analyses to a problem;

- accurately monitoring their own performance;
- retrieving relevant information more effectively.[6]

What is significant is that the research findings on expertise have had little impact on education, despite being widely recognized in sport and occupational areas. This book asks why this is, and takes some first steps towards applying our knowledge of how experts learn to teaching and learning. This includes both how teachers learn to be experts and how students can learn more expertly.

The basic expertise findings are far more ordinary than the mysterious processes of the 'natural talent' approach. They suggest that the key ingredients are:

Opportunities to develop the particular skills. The Mozarts and Beckhams of this world were given exceptional opportunities from an early age – often by a dedicated parent or teacher. Early success then starts a 'multiplier' process that leads to more opportunities that improve the skills even more. Matthew Syed sums this up nicely: 'Child prodigies do not have unusual genes; they have unusual upbringings.'[7]

Strong motivation to be a top performer. Only when individuals want the goal for themselves will the necessary learning take place. Pushy parents and teachers can only help part of the way – but there has to be a hunger from the learner. This also involves being reflective about their performance and adaptive in their response.

Extensive deliberate practice. This research finding[8] has been popularized by Malcolm Gladwell as the 10,000 hours of deliberate practice any top performer will have gone through. Deliberate practice involves practising the things we don't do well in order to improve and involves regular failure as we leave our comfort zone. This practice leads to many of the components in complex

3

skills becoming automatic and includes cognitive development, for example, superior knowledge and memory in the area of their expertise. Here is the expertise paradox: the effortless performance that labels someone 'a natural' is the result of exceptional preparatory effort.

Good coaching and teaching. Top musicians and sports stars invariably give credit to various teachers and role models as key elements in their success. A key part of this is the teacher having a clear sense of progression – what's needed next – and offering skilled and continuous feedback.

So back to Mozart and Beckham; what do they have in common in relation to these basics of expertise?

They started early and had intense parental support. Part of the legend of Mozart was that he was a musical prodigy, composing at 4, performing at 6, and, at 14, able to write out the complete score of Allegri's *Miserere* after hearing it twice. What is less well known is that his father, Leopold, was a highly ambitious music teacher who wrote an acclaimed textbook on teaching violin and who had already taught Mozart's older sister, Nannerl, another child prodigy. It was Leopold who took down and tidied up his son's compositions and who gave up his own composing to concentrate on his son's. He also arranged for money-making tours of Europe for young Mozart, the start of his performance career.

David Beckham's background may be less well known but has remarkable parallels. There is a photograph of a 3-year-old David proudly displaying his new Manchester United shirt, his father being a keen soccer player and avid United fan:

All the strengths in my game are the ones Dad taught me in the park 20 years ago: we'd work on touch and striking the ball properly until it was too dark to see. He'd kick the ball up in the air as high as he could and get me to control it. Then it would be knocking it in with each foot, making sure I was doing it right.[9]

And the famous free kicks?

It was where I started taking free-kicks. After everybody else had finished and was in the social club, I'd stand on the edge of the penalty area and chip a dead ball towards goal. Every time I hit the bar was worth 50p extra pocket money from my dad that week. And, just as important, a pat on the back.

Beckham's father gave up playing himself in order to concentrate on coaching his son and arranging opportunities for him to play:

My parents knew how much I loved football. If there was a way for me to get a game, they did everything they could to make it happen. Whether it was playing or getting coaching, I'd have my chance. I was at every soccer school going. The first one was the Roger Morgan Soccer School, run by the former Spurs winger. I went there over and over again, doing all the badges until I got the gold.

Like Mozart, he was soon performing in public. At age 11 his grandfather funded him to go, for a second time, to the Bobby Charlton Soccer School in Manchester. Competing against much older boys, he won the ball skills competition in front of a 40,000 crowd who had come for a United match. Like the novelty of seeing the 7-year-old Mozart perform, Beckham was usually the youngest and smallest performer on the pitch, a surprising source of such power and skill. But it was no surprise when, at 14, he was put on the books at Manchester United. (He signed the contract with the pen Sir Alex Ferguson had given him when he was 11 – good mentoring from Sir Alex.) You'll know most of the story from then on, but here's Sir Alex's comment:

> David Beckham is Britain's finest striker of a football not because of God-given talent but because he practises with a relentless application that the vast majority of less gifted players wouldn't contemplate.[10]

Both were highly motivated. The arduous practice regimes that both of them underwent seem to have been a source of pleasure. Mozart's composing seems to have been on his own initiative and come as a surprise to his father, who then helped to develop it. David Beckham's account of his childhood is of seeking every opportunity to kick a ball, and being fortunate to have a nearby park where he could play 'with boys twice my age' for hours at a time.

We'll return to the theme of practice being strenuous yet seen as a source of pleasure and satisfaction. It appears in the accounts that many top performers have given, for example, the chess-playing Polgar sisters and the tennis-playing Williams sisters. It does not mean that it was always fun – deliberate practice involves doing what we are not good at till we get good. Developing expertise also involves a single-mindedness that has been a feature of scientific and artistic genius.

Both recorded thousands of hours of purposeful practice. Michael Howe has estimated that Leopold Mozart's arduous and unusual practice regime for his son began when Mozart was 3 years old and involved three hours a day – some 3500 hours by age 6, when the performing tours began. Given that much practice, it was not the quality of playing that made Mozart exceptional; it was that the performer was so young. In an age in which most children did not start learning to play until later than this, his was seen as a rare and God-given talent. Anders Ericsson has called this *the iceberg illusion:*

when we see an extraordinary performance, we do not notice that it is the product of a submerged process involving thousands of hours of practice.[11]

We have seen already how David Beckham clocked up thousands of hours of practice as a child. This was not aimless 'kicking a ball around': much of his practice was with adults and older children who made relatively few allowances for his being younger and small even for his age. He was also a member of several very successful teams, which meant he had had that extensive experience of competitive matches by the time he was a teenager. Though he went to a rugby-playing secondary school, a group of soccer-playing pupils persuaded their physical education teacher to set up a soccer team. He was responsive and this team went on to win various competitions – a good example of the book's theme of teachers recognizing students' interests and building on them.

The importance of purposeful practice is a central theme of this book. We shall see how it is this, rather than some innate skill, that distinguishes top musicians from good musicians. Stories of top performers invariably include practice regimes far more demanding than those of others – the 'first there, last away' from training of such as Beckham.

Both received good coaching and teaching. Both Mozart and Beckham received some of the best teaching that was available. Mozart's early fame meant that he worked with other musical luminaries, for example, J.C. Bach, the son of J.S. Bach. As a result Mozart's early symphonies borrowed heavily from J.S. Bach's work and style.[12] (The young Beethoven, who was subjected to a far more brutal training regime by his own father, later came to Vienna in the hope of working with Mozart but this did not work out – but he did later get teaching there from Haydn and Salieri.) This does not devalue Mozart's early achievements; a vital part of any apprenticeship is to imitate the work of more skilled experts before developing one's own distinctive contribution.

In a similar fashion David Beckham benefited from top-level coaching from an early age, both through local, county and professional club teams.

Part of his apprenticeship was, in the words of his coach at Manchester United, 'to watch the man playing in your position. One day you're going to take his place.' (For those interested, Bryan Robson, Beckham's 'all-time hero', was that player.)

It's not about parents; it's about opportunities. The impression given by this comparison is that becoming a top performer is dependent on inheriting parents devoted to their offspring's success. While there is no shortage of these in both sport and music, opportunities can come from very different sources.

The scientist Rosalind Franklin, whose contribution to discovering the DNA double helix has increasingly been recognized (Crick and Watson obtained, without her knowledge, vital data from her research), and who was a world leader on the molecular structure of viruses, wanted to be a scientist from the age of 15. Even by that age she was an avid astronomer and duly passed her entrance examinations to Cambridge, but her father refused to let her go because he disapproved of university education for women – this was 1938. This led to a major domestic row in which her mother and aunt threatened to support her themselves. He backed down, but his support was always grudging – as was Rosalind's response. We learn more of her later, but this was hardly a dedicated and doting dad.[13]

Matthew Syed, the former three-times British table tennis champion, recounts how he came from a family in which his parents had no interest in table tennis beyond putting a table in the garage. While Matthew and his brother would play on it for hours, the key 'multiplier' was a local club and a local teacher. The club was a small hut with one table that was open 24 hours a day; the teacher was a local primary school teacher 'with a disdain for conventional teaching methods and a passion for sport that bordered on the fanatical'.[14] He was a top national coach and gathered a group of players from the school, who then based themselves at the club.

As a result, for a period in the 1980s, one small neighbourhood in the town of Reading produced more outstanding table tennis players, male and female, than the rest of the nation combined – many of them from the same street. There are many other parallels to this: Kenyan long distance runners from the same Eldoret region, Russian women tennis players from the same Spartak club and British cyclists from Manchester.

This is also the case in other spheres. There would be little disagreement about the artistic talent of Michelangelo, he of the Sistine Chapel and the iconic *Pieta*. In his case it was the opportunities provided by the remarkable culture of fifteenth-century Florence. It was here, at a time of great prosperity and stability, that craft guilds developed. Michelangelo, a beneficiary of this guild system, from age 6 to 10 lived with a stonecutter and his family, learning how to handle a hammer and chisel. Schooling came afterwards and was a brief and unhappy episode. He was then apprenticed to the eminent Ghirlandraio where he learned the skills of sketching, copying and preparing frescoes in one of Florence's largest churches. Then he was taught by the master sculptor Bertoldo. He went on to produce the *Pieta* at age 24. When he was hailed as a genius for this work, his response was, 'If people knew how hard I had to work to gain my mastery, it would not seem so wonderful at all.'[15]

Jessica Ennis, the heptathlon gold medal winner and 'face of Britain' in the 2012 Olympics, tells a similar story of the dedication and effort involved in honing her skills in seven events. Her opportunities came through a local holiday athletics camp in Sheffield at which the undersized teenager, bullied at school, found something she enjoyed and was encouraged in by the coaching staff. This led to a demanding training routine 'slogging your guts out on a wet and windy track while receiving barbs and brickbats'.[16] By age 17 she was training every night and competing at weekends ('it was relentless'), which meant her social life was severely restricted. But there were enough successes ('multipliers') to sustain this punishing schedule, so exacting that she missed the Beijing Olympics through injury. The result was a momentous gold medal in London in 2012.

Ability myths

Why has so little of this knowledge of expertise permeated educational thinking, especially when it is widely recognized elsewhere? This book argues that this is largely because much of education is still steeped in *ability myths*, the cultural heritage of much Anglo-Saxon thinking about intelligence. We don't now talk much about IQs in schools because of the doubtful past of IQ testing and its exponents. However, we are willing to talk about ability, aptitude and the gifted and talented as if these are very different concepts.

A good example of this in England is the commercially produced Cognitive Abilities Test (CATS) taken by over two-thirds of 11-year-olds on entry into secondary school. This is little more than a repackaged intelligence test, with verbal, non-verbal and numerical sections. These provide ability scores and form the basis of predictions for how well students should do in exams at 16, against which student progress is then tracked.

Such results are reasonable indicators of *developed* cognitive ability, how students have responded to education, but can easily be misinterpreted as a measure of *fixed ability* – the underlying cause of their educational achievement, rather than a product of it. Labelling children as high or low ability runs the risk of seeing their potential as fixed. Susan Hart and colleagues in their *Learning Without Limits* have shown how '"ability labelling" exerts an active, powerful force within school and classroom processes, helping to create the very disparities of achievement that it purports to explain'.[17]

This challenge to ability myths is developed in the next chapter, but for the moment the key litmus-test questions for the reader are as follows:

- Can we give somebody ability?
- Can we improve someone's intelligence?

Predictably, I will be arguing 'yes' to both questions (as have Bill Lucas and Guy Claxton in *New Kinds of Smart* in this series[18]) and looking at how we might do this. However, I recognize that many of us carry cultural baggage originating in the assumptions of such as Francis Galton and Cyril Burt about intelligence being inherited and fixed.

Getting ability

Nobody is born an accomplished anything, though you would not guess this from some of the language we use. We have 'born tennis players', talent 'wired into the genes' and skills 'touched by God'. I am treading a tightrope here; I am not claiming we are all born blank slates for the environment to write on (as B.F. Skinner and the radical behaviourists did[19]), but I am rejecting claims that specific abilities are 'hard-wired' at birth. One of the features of human development is how much we have to learn. We are, for example, born with a capacity for language, but the language we speak, and how well we speak it, are the product of learning in a particular environment. Our distinctive strength as a species is the generality of these capacities, their *plasticity*, which then allow so much flexibility in how they are expressed. This allows us to be far more adaptive than other species, much of whose behaviour is genetically laid down as fixed-response patterns.

This still leaves open the question of why some are so much better than others at particular skills. It is clear that some children walk and talk earlier than others, even in the same family. Is it quicker reaction times that mark out the child sports star, or the capacity to pick up a tune that identifies the future musician? The evidence suggests it is much more complex than this. One key factor is how a small initial advantage, for example, when and where we were born, can lead to a series of *multipliers* that rapidly widen the skills gap. You are a bit more coordinated than I am, so kick a ball better, which means you are put in the practice squad while I do basics. The squad produces a team that has regular coaching. It does well and gets more intensive coaching and bigger matches. You go on to a representative side and serious coaching, and so on. Soon you are a competitive 'natural talent' and I just kick the ball around in friendlies. It's back to Beckham.

This may seem a bit too easy as an explanation. But how do you explain the following?:

- Bill Gates, Paul Allen (Microsoft), Steve Jobs (Apple), Eric Schmidt (Novell, Google) and Bill Joy (Sun Microsystems) were all born within two years of each other in the mid-1950s.

- Forty per cent of top Canadian ice hockey players are born between January and March and a further 30 per cent are born in April to June.[20]

- Summer-born children in England are likely to lag behind winter-born children in their academic performances right through to university level.

- Summer-born children are more likely to be identified as having special needs.[21]

Without giving too much away now, the answers are not to do with astrology.

Opportunities and interactions

Multipliers make their impact through the opportunities that are available and the quality of the interactions with those who are more skilled. We can look at two levels of multipliers: social and individual. Social multipliers stem from a culture, or subculture, in which possessing certain skills are socially necessary or valued. We now live in an age in which many children are more skilled than their parents when it comes to using mobile phone technology. Where there are strong musical traditions, for example, Celtic, Appalachian and Maritime Canadian, it is a given that most children will learn to play instruments. Being able to ski is an expectation in Switzerland, as is swimming in Australia and running in the Kenyan Highlands. We are not surprised when these cultures produce many skilled performers – the opportunities and the multipliers are in place.

How *individual multipliers* operate is far more complex. Given the right opportunities, what seems vital is the effect of the *interaction* with those who are teaching the skills. I emphasize the interaction because what works for one individual may have a negative impact on another. Reading about the early years of some child prodigies, it is hard to imagine how they produced such positive outcomes. Beethoven, at age 4, was regularly beaten by his father, his music teacher, during his clavier and violin lessons. He was also made to get up and practise at midnight, when his alcoholic father staggered home. Not the recipe, we might think, for a lifelong passion for music, yet, in terms of musical response, this boot-camp approach seems to have been productive. This may partly be because he had a supportive mother and soon moved on to other, more constructive, teachers.

Other stories seem bizarre rather than cruel. At a few months old Tiger Woods was plonked in his high chair in the garage to watch his father hit endless golf practice shots. His father fashioned special golf clubs for young Tiger so that he was out on the golf course by age 2 and appeared on TV aged 3 to demonstrate his prowess at hitting a golf ball. When Tiger was practising a shot, his father would creep up behind and shout just as he was about to hit the ball – early practice on concentrating and ignoring crowd noises. However bizarre, for this individual, the interaction was, clearly productive and positive in terms of golf expertise.

13

These examples represent the hot-housing of top performers. Most of us have neither the desire nor the means to work this way and we may need to be reassured that there are other, slower ways of developing ability. We may need reminding that geniuses such as Charles Darwin, Marie Curie and Albert Einstein took their time in arriving at world-changing contributions, as did best-selling author Mary Wesley, who was 71 when her first of many novels for adults was published. The basic principle remains the same. It was sustained and single-minded application that led to their contributions. They put in their 10,000 hours – and much, much more.

While many received encouragement, some had to battle against opposition. This has been particularly true for many women. Mary Anne Evans had to publish as 'George Eliot' and, as we shall see, Marie Curie received little or no support for years. Rosalind Franklin, whom we met earlier, had to do much of her work alone and was barred from some grants because she was a woman. She was not even allowed to eat with men in the (male) common room or go to the male-only bar at King's College London where the scientists met and talked.

The expert teacher

Expert learning needs expert teachers, and to become expert teachers we need to be expert learners ourselves. So the book's *The Expert Learner* title is deliberately ambiguous: it's about both the learner and the teacher. As in other professions, teaching expertise is the product of using experience to develop powerful frameworks in which to make sense of both familiar and unfamiliar information.

The psychologist Gary Klein provides the real-life example of a team of firefighters called to a house fire.[22] The fire is in the back in the kitchen area. The team hose water onto the fire, but it just roars back. They retreat and then try again, with the same result. The experienced commander realizes that something is not right and orders his men to leave. At this point the floor on which they had been standing collapses into the basement fire below.

Why did the commander pull his men out when he did? He didn't know why, and others quickly put it down to extrasensory perception. Klein spent hours of conversation trying to tease out why he had made this sudden decision. He realized that the commander had done what experts do; he had used his experience to develop a mental framework with which to make sense of the properties of the fire scene quickly without too much conscious thought. This allowed him to recognize something was amiss. He did not know the house had a basement, but he had sensed the fire was too hot and too quiet for a kitchen fire.

This is a dramatic example, but in less dramatic circumstances expert teachers are interpreting daily what is happening in each classroom they work in. Entering a deathly quiet classroom may seem like a wonderful moment for a novice teacher; for the expert teacher it will set alarm bells ringing – is there a hidden drama going on in the room that could erupt at any moment? Why do medical experts see more in a patient's data than other doctors? What do they look for that others don't notice?

I also use *expert sports coaching* as a model for skilled classroom interaction. Sport has been chosen because, like teaching, no two situations are ever the same. This means that the coach has to be highly adaptable. We also know that top coaches set clear standards and goals and are able to draw on a large repertoire of techniques and moves. The skill is in choosing the most productive way to progress learning. This also includes giving continuous and effective feedback.

The organization of this book

A refrain in this book is the need to understand 'the big picture'. So here's an overview of how this book is organized:

Chapter 1 does some ground-clearing around ability assumptions in education. I start here because these culturally embedded beliefs undermine what we know about expertise and the development of ability. Ability is *malleable* and therefore open to development. This leads to questions about the way ability labels are used in education.

Chapter 2 summarizes what we know about the process of expert learning, drawing on a range of examples from different domains, including chess, music, science, sport and medicine. The intention is to draw out the key characteristics of expert learning.

In Chapters 3 to 7 the key expertise findings are applied to teaching and learning in education. While the focus is often on classrooms in schools, the findings can be applied to a much broader range of educational provision, so 'classroom' is a proxy for other educational settings, for example, colleges, vocational and occupational training, in which there may also be some different instructional approaches. These chapters are organized around the key concepts of Assessment for Learning, an approach with which many teachers in the UK and other countries will be familiar. This is essentially about informal classroom assessment in which evidence is gathered to 'identify where learners are in their learning, where they need to go and how best to get there'.[23] As we'll see, this aligns well with some of the key elements of expertise: skilled diagnostics, clear goal setting, and effective feedback.

Chapter 3 addresses the expertise messages of having high expectations and goals and the need for effective 'mental frameworks'. It focuses on expectations, learner identity and motivation. What are we asking of our students and do we expect too little, particularly of the more disadvantaged? The chapter considers the problems of labelling learners, how we can encourage deeper approaches to learning, and how we can motivate students to take on more challenging demands.

Chapter 4 develops the idea that experts develop powerful mental frameworks. These allow them to organize and integrate information more effectively. This is true of expert teachers, who are then able to communicate this to their students. At the heart of this is making clear the learning intentions and what success looks like. The emphasis here is on learners being clear about what they are learning and why, so that they can make sense of it for themselves, a vital element in deeper learning approaches.

If we are to make realistic learning demands on our students, we need to know what they can do already. Chapter 5 looks at how experts arrive at diagnostic decisions in medicine and other occupations. This is then applied to the classroom: how do teachers make decisions about learning and find out where their students are in their learning? The importance of classroom interaction, particularly oral, is seen as a key diagnostic element.

Getting good feedback is an essential part of how experts learn. In Chapter 6 we look at what makes feedback effective, drawing particularly on sports coaching expertise. The chapter develops the key elements that allow feedback to close the gap between where learners are and where they need to get to.

The final chapter considers the implications of what we know about how experts learn for schools. Given that opportunities are critical to expert learning, what is the role of the school, college or training institution? We look at the culture of the school and the importance to having its own vision, of providing opportunities for all learners, and of support for individual learners. In what ways does a school act as a *social multiplier* and make the high demands that lead to more effective learning? How is deliberate practice encouraged? How reflective are a school's leadership, its teachers and its students?

At the end of each of these chapters I provide questions and activities on the main themes. The intention is to encourage further discussion about what the findings are, and how they can be applied in the readers' own situations.

1

Nothing's Fixed: Tackling Ability Myths

In the modern world, the conception of abilities as fixed or even as predetermined is an anachronism.

(Robert Sternberg[24])

As soon as we announce someone is a 'born tennis player', has 'God-given musical ability' or is a 'natural', we have a problem. This is the assumption that this talent is something that the person was endowed with at birth, which then unfolds, often at an early age. Lurking in this is the belief that most of us were not born with this level of natural ability, and so are restricted in what we can achieve. This chapter tackles these widely held *ability myths*, which are still found in educational thinking.

Why am I fussing about inborn ability in a book about expertise? Because belief in it undermines what we know about expert learning and has a negative effect on education, both in terms of policy and what goes on in the classroom. So, for example, siren calls for more selection assume that if we can identify our 'gifted and talented', then we can offer them an enriched learning environment. The rest, the ungifted and untalented, must make do with a stodgier diet. The evidence from America's current high-stakes accountability testing programme ('No Child Left Behind') is strong on this – the lowest attaining and most disadvantaged get the worst teaching, consisting of dull test drills in the basics, to crank up their test scores.[25] This is a negative *school multiplier effect*, as good students will get more imaginative teaching and enjoy learning more, whereas those who struggle may get dull basics and be itching to leave education behind.

Why write about ability rather than intelligence or aptitude? Because in polite society we do not now talk much about IQ because of its historical baggage, yet we are happy to talk loosely about low and high ability, even about having no ability. David Gillborn and Deborah Youdell have called ability 'the new IQism', which:

> acts as an *unrecognized* version of 'intelligence' and 'IQ'. If we were to substitute 'IQ' for 'ability' many alarm bells would ring that currently remain silent because 'ability' acts as an untainted yet powerful reconstitution of all the beliefs previously wrapped up in terms such as intelligence.[26]

They are right. Much of the ability talk I hear in schools might as well be about IQ scores and carries the same message about fixed ability. As we shall see later, our beliefs about ability powerfully shape how we view our students, and their own views of their abilities shape how they learn.

> "Ability acts as an *unrecognized* version of 'intelligence' and 'IQ'. If we were to substitute 'IQ' for 'ability' many alarm bells would ring that currently remain silent because 'ability' acts as an untainted yet powerful reconstitution of all the beliefs previously wrapped up in terms such as intelligence." – David Gillborn and Deborah Youdell

19

Where does aptitude fit in?

I don't make a big distinction between ability and aptitude, which is treated as a specific ability. The same talent argument applies: aptitude is developed, not inborn. When we select for aptitude, we don't select those who have never played music or sport or who have never done any maths; we select those who show promise in what they have done already. For some, like athlete Jessica Ennis, it may only have been a taster to which they responded well, suggesting potential, but it can never be assessed without some experience. Would you assess someone's aptitude for swimming without ever going near water?

Ability myths

The *ability myths* tackled here are that ability is something:

- we are born with (or without) as part of our genetic inheritance;
- child prodigies have a prodigious amount of;
- that doesn't change much over time.

This book's alternative way of thinking about ability is that:

- genes play a far less direct role than historically assumed; it is the *interplay* of genes and the environment that is critical;
- 'genius' is the result of what has been achieved rather than of spotting promise;

- ability is developed over time, and high ability needs unusual levels of motivation and practice.

Inheriting ability

The intention of this section is to review some deeply held cultural assumptions around inborn ability and to consider alternative approaches. I devote space to this because our cultural heritage often provides our default position on talent and ability. Even when we have consciously moved to a more informed position, we may find that, when scratched, we move back to seeing some as 'born with it' and others who 'just don't have it'. Here I briefly review some of the key arguments used in support of innate ability as well as some contrary evidence.[27] Genes are important, but they do not work in the inflexible way previously assumed; their expression is both malleable and dependent on their interplay with the environment.

An extremely brief cultural history of inherited ability

Some of us will heartily have sung the well-known nineteenth-century children's hymn 'All things bright and beautiful', which includes the following:

The rich man in his castle,
The poor man at his gate,
He made them, high or lowly,
And ordered their estate.

Without getting too sociologically embroiled, this social class-based view of destiny was the basis for assumptions about intelligence for the nineteenth

21

and twentieth centuries. It was not a big step for such as Francis Galton (1822–1911), the source of much of our cultural legacy about intelligence, to declare that it was inherited and those of high social status were endowed with more of it. So direct was the genetic transmission of intelligence, and so closely related to social class, that Galton coined the term 'eugenics' and proposed that the breeding of the lower classes should be restricted. Galton's work was continued in England by statisticians such as Charles Spearman (1863–1945), who developed factor analysis techniques that supported the idea of a single general intelligence factor (g), and Cyril Burt (1883–1971). Burt's importance was in his role in shaping the English secondary education system in the 1944 Education Act, with its tripartite division of schools (grammar, technical, secondary modern) and the use of 11+ selection tests, many of which he designed. Around three-quarters of 11-year-olds would fail the 11+. In Patricia Broadfoot's haunting judgement, 'Intelligence testing, as a mechanism for social control, was unsurpassed in teaching the doomed majority that failure was the result of their own inbuilt inadequacy.'[28]

> "Intelligence testing, as a mechanism for social control, was unsurpassed in teaching the doomed majority that failure was the result of their own inbuilt inadequacy." – Patricia Broadfoot

Contrast Burt's own view of this:

> It should be an essential part of the child's education to teach him how to take a possible beating on the 11+ (or any other examination), just as he should learn to take a beating in a half mile race, or in a bout with boxing gloves, or a football match with a rival school.[29]

So speaks a man who, after training from an early age, was victorious – his father teaching him Latin declensions 'morning by morning while still in my cot'. Somehow he also managed to square all this with being the psychologist in charge of special education in London.

These men, and their counterparts in America, all came to the study of intelligence with a particular social agenda, which they then justified through their 'scientific' statistical work. Their core belief was that intelligence was inborn and fixed, with some races having more than others (guess the order). Here's Burt again: 'This general intellectual factor, appears to be inherited, or at least inborn. Neither knowledge nor practice, neither interest nor industry, will avail to increase it.'[30]

Were these psychologists simply products of their time? Here's Alfred Binet, the French creator of the first intelligence tests, castigating

[those] recent thinkers who seem to have given their moral support to these deplorable verdicts by affirming that an individual's intelligence is a fixed quantity, a quantity that cannot be increased. We must protest and react against this brutal pessimism; we must try to demonstrate it is founded upon nothing.[31]

For Binet, who had different cultural values, the aim of intelligence testing was to identify those having difficulties so that they could be helped, given he was responsible for special education in Paris. His goal was to improve learning, through what he called 'mental orthopaedics', and we might call 'learning how to learn', so students could improve their learning skills:

It is in this practical sense, the only one accessible to us, that we say that the intelligence of these children has been increased. We have increased what constitutes the intelligence of a pupil, the capacity to learn and assimilate instruction.[32]

23

Binet is the starting point of this book's alternative approach to ability. The basic assumption is that we can improve ability/intelligence. Ability is *malleable*, not fixed.

So what part do genes play in ability?

There is increasing agreement that arguments about 'nature versus nurture', with fixed percentages allocated to each, have had their day. We now recognize that it is the *interaction* of our genes with the environment that is critical, and this will vary according to the situation. There is a genetic factor in height; tall parents have taller children than shorter parents, but the environment will play a crucial role in how this is expressed. So, for example, over a 50-year period Japanese children reared in California were, on average, over a foot taller than children raised in Japan.[33] Studies of cognitive development suggest that heritability plays only a minor role when children are growing up in a disadvantaged environment, because it's the environment that largely determines the levels of development.[34]

Heritability confusions. When we read that height is 75 per cent inherited, do we interpret this as meaning three-quarters of my height comes from my genes, and the environment is responsible for a further quarter? This would be wrong. Heritability applies to a group, not an individual, and measures the variation within this group – so the 75 per cent is only of the *differences* in height. So if we talk of intelligence being 50 per cent inherited, we are talking only about the differences between scores within a specific group, not the total score. So, for example, even though having two ears is genetically determined, heritability is virtually zero because there is little or no variance within the population. We nearly all have two ears, yet in the 1950s wearing earrings had high heritability – those wearing them had mainly XX chromosomes (women) while those without had mainly XY chromosomes (men).[35] These (silly) examples remind us that heritability is easy to misunderstand and, because it is based on correlations, never tells us about the causes of differences.

What we are realizing is that genes do have an important role, but this is much less direct, and far more complex, than is often assumed. Any claim that there is a gene 'for' maths, happiness or schizophrenia is guilty of misleading oversimplification.[36] What we now know is that complex behaviours are multiply determined and that it is how genes are *expressed* that counts.[37] So, for example, we are born with the capacity for developing complex language, but whether we learn to speak, how sophisticated our speech is, and what language we speak, are all down to interplay with the environment.

> "Genes do have an important role, but this is much less direct, and far more complex, than is often assumed. Any claim that there is a gene 'for' maths, happiness or schizophrenia is guilty of misleading oversimplification. What we now know is that complex behaviours are multiply determined and that it is how genes are *expressed* that counts."

Inherited does not mean immutable. The unhelpful image of a *genetic blueprint* also feeds into misunderstandings of heredity. The mistake here is to see genetic patterns as *immutable* when in fact they can be modified. David Shenk offers us a more helpful image, one of a giant *control board* in every cell in the body (giant because we are dealing with over 20,000 genes in every cell) in which the genes are like volume knobs and switches. These can be turned up/down/on/off by another gene or by miniscule environmental inputs. This is a continuous and active interaction from conception onwards and supports the claim that we develop, rather than inherit, traits. A powerful example here is the inherited condition of phenylketonuria (PKU), a defect that can cause severe mental retardation. Newborns are now immediately tested for this because an immediate change of diet can prevent the mutant DNA being expressed.[38] Stephen Gould makes the point that:

the truly salient issues are malleability and flexibility, not fallacious parsing by percentages. A trait may be 90 percent heritable yet entirely malleable. A twenty dollar pair of eyeglasses . . . may fully correct a defect in vision that is 100 percent heritable.[39]

What do twin studies tell us?

The early nature–nurture debates were often focused on twin studies, particularly identical twins separated at birth. There was good reason for this – here is a perfect natural experiment: find identical twins who were separated at birth and raised in different environments and we will be able to measure how much they have in common. Because they have identical genes that will tell us how much these have influenced development – what is the same despite different nurture. All very neat in theory, but messier in reality since very few identical twins are separated at birth and brought up in different environments.[40]

There is a public fascination with the similarities between separated identical twins, an example being the 'Jim twins', who got national coverage on US TV, which in turn led to the funding of a large-scale research programme by Thomas Bouchard. The box below summarizes some of the striking similarities of the Jim twins.

The surprising similarities of the separated Jim twins[41]

The Jim twins were born in 1940 in Ohio and separated at four weeks of age. They met again at age 39 and it was like looking in a mirror. They looked the same and talked the same and their lives uncannily resembled each other. Not only were they both called Jim but they:

- both had married and divorced a woman named Linda and then married a woman called Betty;

- each had an adopted brother called Larry and a childhood dog named Toy;

- liked maths but disliked spelling in school;

- named their firstborn James Alan and James Allen;

- each smoked Salem cigarettes and drank Miller Lite;

- enjoyed carpentry and mechanical drawing;

- chewed their nails, had migraines and served as part-time sheriffs in their respective towns;

- drove the same model car, lived in the same region of Ohio and vacationed in Florida;

- were 6 feet tall and weighed 180 pounds.

Is this not a remarkable story with which to illustrate the power of genes? The media coverage certainly thought so. But if we take a step back, we may want to be a bit more cautious about what we read into it. For example, what have your genes to do with the name your adoptive parents gave you, or the naming of children, dogs and the choosing of Bettys and Lindas? The same goes for the same tastes in cigarettes, beer, cars and holidays. Is there mileage in the alternative explanation that if you both grow up in small-town blue-collar Ohio (as they both did), you are likely to finish up, along with many others, with similar tastes in names, beers, cars and cigarettes? The point here is that if we look for similarities, we can find them, and we can also ignore differences, of which there were many. Twin studies mean we cannot ignore genetic contributions, but we can also read too much into them and underestimate the interaction with the environment.

27

The Flynn effect[42]

One of the strongest challenges to the inherited ability argument is the increase over time in intelligence scores. James Flynn found that intelligence test scores have improved far too quickly over time to be explained in terms of genetic changes. His explanation, which sits comfortably with the claims here about expertise, is that the improvement over time was largely the result of *social multipliers*. The two key multipliers for him are the educational emphasis on:

- scientific concepts and abstract classifications;
- the encouragement of 'on-the-spot problem solving without a previously learned method'.[43]

These multipliers encourage the very kind of thinking many IQ subtests require. He provides a trivial, but telling, example of similarities: 'What do dogs and rabbits have in common?' Our grandparents may have given a functional response – you use dogs to hunt rabbits. The required answer is 'They are mammals', for our grandparents a big 'So what?' Ten-year-olds today would recognize this answer, even though most might have gone for a more concrete answer ('four legs').

How do you explain child prodigies and savants?

When we see someone very young doing something very remarkable, it is very easy to conclude they were born with a special talent. So when Mozart played in public at age 6, there could be no other explanation than that he had 'been touched by God'. The same goes for Michael Jackson (though a lesser god?). Tiger Woods is on TV at 3 while Susan Polgar, whom we will learn more about in Chapter 2, wins the first chess competition she enters at age

5, half the age of the other competitors, is world female under-16 champion at age 12 and becomes the first female grandmaster when she was 22.

'Natural talent' seems such an obvious explanation at this point, especially if we don't look too closely at what has gone before each of these impressive debuts. As mentioned earlier, Anders Ericsson has warned us about the *iceberg illusion* – paying attention to the visible and not to the far bigger base that underpins it. Michael Howe observes that prodigies 'have almost always received very considerable help and encouragement prior to the time at which their ability has been seen to be remarkable'.[44]

None of this denies that child prodigies are remarkable, and looking at how they learned their skills simply increases our admiration of them. Taking the easy route and declaring they are different from the rest of us as a result of inborn talents does not do justice to their efforts. What we should be in awe of is young Mozart's musical output. David Shenk points out that what are recognized as his great works, for example, Symphony no. 29, came some ten years after his first symphonies, while his first great piano concerto, no. 9, *Jeunehomme*, written at age 21, was his 271st completed composition. His first operatic masterpiece, *Idomeneo*, was his thirteenth opera.

Mozart felt this lack of recognition for his efforts. In a letter to his father he wrote:

> People make a great mistake who think that my art has come easily to me, nobody has devoted so much time and thought to composition as I . . . there is not a famous master whose work I have studied over and over.[45]

So much for effortless mastery.

> 66 People make a great mistake who think that my art has come easily to me, nobody has devoted so much time and thought to composition as I . . . there is not a famous master whose work I have studied over and over. 99 – Amadeus Mozart

What about savants?

We are all aware that there are individuals who, sometimes from an early age, can perform remarkable feats of memory or calculation, which defy normal explanation.

Kim Peek: a prodigious savant[46]

In the Oscar-winning film *Rain Man*, Dustin Hoffman's Raymond Babbitt was modelled on Kim Peek, a man who:

- had memorized the contents of over 12,000 books word for word;
- had encyclopaedic knowledge of geography, sports, music and 14 other areas;
- could speed-read books, with understanding, two pages at a time (one eye on each), with the pages either way up;
- was severely cognitively disabled, scored badly on IQ tests and could not button his own shirt;
- could do complex mental calculations; for example, he would tell questioners the day of the week on which they would turn 65, yet he could not work out how much he would have change from a dollar if he spent 50 cents ('about 70 cents').

What we know about savants is that they are individuals with exceptional ability in one or more fields that coexists with some form of disability, many of whom are on the autistic spectrum – the syndrome occurring in as many as one in ten autistic persons. These skills range from very particular 'splinter' skills, for example, remembering train timetables, through 'talented' savants who have one area of expertise, for example, music, to 'prodigious' savants with several or multiple areas of expertise. A common feature across the spectrum is a prodigious memory.

So what kind of support do the hundred plus savants studied provide for individual inborn ability? Very little, I suggest, since the research indicates that the development of these extraordinary talents is more of a challenge to our understanding of the neurology of the brain and how the mind works than it is to genetics. This is because these abilities appear to be the product of overcompensation in one part of the brain for developmental deficits in another, bypassing the normal integration of the two parts. This may produce a radically different way of processing information, which may be a cause of the prodigious memory common to all savants.

So, rather than seeing the talents of the savant as genetically hard-wired, it seems more appropriate to view them as the results of alternative wiring, which has resulted from the need to compensate for faulty development. Darold Treffert, the leading expert on the savant syndrome, has described this in terms of *rewiring, recruitment and release*. The rewiring and recruitment are the setting up of alternative processing channels, for example, right hemisphere drawing to compensate for a lack of language caused by the left hemisphere developmental problems often implicated in autism. 'Release' is the most puzzling mechanism, since this involves the opening up of dormant capacities in the brain for new, and often surprising, skills. The evidence for this comes from those savants, almost half of those known, whose powers developed after injury or disease, for example, elderly persons with frontal-temporal dementia who show art and musical composition abilities, several at a prodigious level, as the dementia proceeds. No such interest or talent was evident before the beginning of the dementia process. And here's another to stretch credulity: a 54-year-old surgeon gets

31

struck by lightning and survives. He then develops an obsessive interest in classical music, learns to play the piano and has a recurrent tune in his head. This is transcribed into a major sonata, which he now performs professionally.[47]

Most examples involve art and music. In the UK we have Stephen Wiltshire who:

[d]raws lifelike, accurate representations of buildings and cities, sometimes after having only observed them briefly. After a 12 minute helicopter ride over London he drew, in three hours, a totally accurate sketch of an area of four square miles.

Was diagnosed as autistic at age three. He had no language and, at the age of five, was sent to Queensmill Special School in London. Here he had teachers who recognized his remarkable ability to draw from memory and would take him on outings to look at buildings for him to draw later and who entered his work in art competitions.[48]

Other common savant skills are calendar calculating, lightning calculation and mechanical and spatial skills. These skills tend to be right hemisphere in type, with the left hemisphere skills of language and semantic organization of memory often impaired through congenital disability or accident and disease.

The malleable brain

The study of savants challenges our views of how the brain works. Above all, it reinforces claims about the *plasticity* of its processes. If one function is closed down by disability or accident, another may be recruited. Some of the alternative rewirings may be more powerful in some respects, as in the case of the prodigious memory of savants. This indirectly relates to what we know about expertise, that becoming an expert increases specialist memory and that this process modifies the brain. A good example of this is the larger than normal growth of the posterior hippocampus, a region associated with spatial representation, found in London black cab taxi drivers. As part of their training they have to demonstrate 'the knowledge' of London's streets from memory. No one argues that they were genetically 'born to drive cabs': this brain development is a product of experience and increases with it.[49] The same is true for the regions associated with left-hand finger movements in violinists and finger movements in Braille readers.

> "The study of savants challenges our views of how the brain works. Above all, it reinforces claims about the *plasticity* of its processes. If one function is closed down by disability or accident, another may be recruited. Some of the alternative rewirings may be more powerful in some respects, as in the case of the prodigious memory of savants."

Isn't ability/IQ a good predictor of success?

IQ scores, and ability scores from tests such as the widely used Cognitive Abilities Test (CATs) in the UK, are reasonable predictors of academic outcomes. But this does not mean that such ability is the *cause* of these achievements so much as an *indicator* of them. Those who have benefited from education, including what goes on in the home in terms of vocabulary and reasoning, will do well on them, as they are likely to do in school and work. So ability tests are best seen as measures of how much someone has gained from general education. Robert Sternberg makes the point that:

> [w]hat distinguishes ability tests from other kinds of assessments is how the ability tests are used (usually predictively) rather than what

they measure. There is no qualitative distinction among the various kinds of assessment. All tests measure various kinds of developing expertise.[50]

When the results of a 'snapshot' ability test are allowed to determine future chances, the 11+ being a classic example, we have a case of fixed ability thinking's negative effects. Michael Howe asks what would happen if we applied the same logic to the driving test, so that failure was interpreted as a lack of inherited capacity to drive, 'dooming everyone who failed on the first attempt to a lifetime of dependence on public transport'.[51] The other side of the coin is when students are said, with a sniff of disapproval, to have 'overachieved' in an attainment assessment given their ability limits.

Schools develop intelligence

Turning on its head the assumption that inborn ability causes achievement, there is strong evidence that schooling causes ability to improve. We accept this for developed abilities such as literacy and numeracy, yet may still harbour the thought that we can't do much about underlying ability – the sort reflected in IQ tests. However, there is strong evidence that this is exactly what happens, with the improvement of scores on IQ tests linked to the length and quality of education and with decreases in scores resulting from delays and interruptions to education, including summer holidays.[52] Bill Lucas and Guy Claxton have developed this argument in *New Kinds of Smart* in this series.

Top experts do not necessarily have top IQs

The pioneers of intelligence testing assumed that a high score was the basis for high achievement. Lewis Terman, who developed the still widely used Stanford-Binet intelligence test, tried to estimate the IQs of geniuses (Galton came in with a whopping 200[53]). He also went a step further and set up a large-scale longitudinal study to track the success of school students whom he identified as 'exceptionally superior' because they were in the top 1 per cent of IQ scores. Terman was convinced that inherited intelligence was the source of success and that some groups had more than others – he was a eugenicist and worked to restrict immigration to the US of various ethnic groups. Unfortunately for him, the results did not bear his theory out – not only did his 'Termites' do no better than other students from similar backgrounds, but their IQs *dropped* by an average of 10 points over the next 20 years.[54] Few achieved eminence, whereas two future Nobel Prize winners (William Schockley and Louis Alvarez) failed the selection criteria, as did the musicians Isaac Stern and Yehudi Menuhin. A 1984 retrospective of the 60-year study, which followed up on those students with IQs over 180, concluded that 'they were not as remarkable as might have been expected . . . there is the disappointing sense that they may have done more with their lives'.[55]

Straw men?

Your reaction to the arguments in this chapter may be to declare I am attacking straw men – we all know ability is developed and we have moved on from the thinking of the IQ pioneers. I would be pleased if you were right and I am needlessly fighting old wars. If so, what do you make of this 2009 comment from Chris Woodhead, the former Chief Inspector of Schools in England?

> I think it would be unlikely that large numbers of grammar school kids would come from these disadvantaged areas – the genes are likely to be better if your parents are teachers, academics, lawyers, whatever. And the nurture is likely to be better.

Why do we think that we can make him ('not very bright Jimmy') brighter than God made him?[56]

In the rest of the book, and without invoking the Almighty, we see how we can improve Jimmy's abilities.

Questions for discussion

1. Is ability talk an issue in your place of work? If so, what forms does it take?

2. Are there more constructive alternatives to 'fixed ability' language?

3. How is 'ability' used in your school/college documents and systems (streaming/banding, etc.)?

4. Do you have a 'gifted and talented' programme? Is there a better name you could use for this (so that 90 per cent are no longer 'ungifted and untalented')?

5. What other issues has this chapter raised for you?

2

How Experts Learn

It's not that I'm so smart; it's just that I stay with problems longer.

(Albert Einstein)

I hope to do it in time. I myself am very far from satisfied with this but, well, getting better must come through doing it and through trying.

(Vincent van Gogh)

One of the dangers of treating top performers as a species apart is that we do not look systematically at what they can do, or how they learned to do it. We may just treat it as a gift – from God or from genes – and leave it there. Fortunately, there have been those who want to know more and who have investigated how expertise develops. Like any good scientist, they have wanted to know the *how* of what goes on, in their case, in top performance. And, like scientific discoveries, this does not remove the awe we feel when we learn about what lies behind a great performance. Discoveries about the structure of matter lead to a

> **"**Like scientific discoveries, this does not remove the awe we feel when we learn about what lies behind a great performance. Discoveries about the structure of matter lead to a greater sense of wonder than just accepting that matter is a given.**"**

greater sense of wonder than just accepting that matter is a given – hence the current excitement around the Higgs Boson particle. The same is true for talent.

The systematic study of expertise began with the skills of chess, music and sports, skills often used as examples of natural gifts. In this chapter we look at what has been learned from these and other studies of expertise.

Learning from grandmasters

The 1950s produced systematic studies of chess expertise and these have continued to this day. This is partly because expertise in chess is relatively easy to define, your expertise is signalled by your ranking; a grandmaster is, by definition, a top performer. Because chess is such a restricted activity and has such a rich record of moves and games, this is ideal for systematic experimentation. What does a grandmaster do differently to a novice? Do they think differently? What would your next move be in this game – and how does it compare with what experts have done in the same situation?

Chess has also influenced psychologists in developing models of artificial intelligence as they sought to understand the way the human mind processes information. One of the most dramatic outcomes of this was the 1996 chess series between world champion Garry Kasparov and the giant IBM Deep Blue computer. In this contest the limited processing powers of the human brain were pitched against a computer capable of processing 100 million positions a second. Yet Kasparov won the initial series and it was only when an even more powerful computer, processing 200 million positions a second and programmed by a chess expert, was introduced, that the computer won (2–1 with 3 draws).[57]

What have we learned from chess? Three key ideas about learning can be derived from chess expertise:

1. We are far more effective learners when we understand what we are doing – the big picture – and can approach problems at a deeper 'principled' level.

2. We are capable of remembering more than we think.

3. Chess skills are learned and are limited in scope. Nobody is born a chess player, and chess grandmasters' everyday skills are often remarkably ordinary away from the chessboard.

Seeing and understanding the big picture

Figure 1 is a well-replicated example of chess memory. You are asked to study the 24-piece chess game below for five seconds and to remember as many of the pieces, in their correct places, as you can. The board is then covered and you set out the pieces on another board. You would then be given a further series of five-second exposures until you had placed them all correctly. As a quick mental exercise, how many pieces can you correctly recall from the first five-second look?

I will use the research evidence to estimate what might have happened. On the first exposure

- novice and non-chess players will typically remember 3 to 5 pieces and take around 5 more looks to place at least 20 pieces accurately;

- good chess players would remember around 8 pieces and take two more looks to get to 20 pieces;

Figure 1 Memory for chess piece placings

- grandmasters remember around 16 after five seconds and after one more exposure would have 20 in place. After one or two more looks, the grandmaster will have them all in place.

For those of us who are novices, how did we remember our five pieces? Just go for the top row or two, spot similar pieces (e.g. the castles) or focus on a group of pieces? If we don't know the names of the pieces, we then have to make up names and stories to help us remember (a horse staring at an ashtray in the top left?). So how do grandmasters remember so many pieces?

1. They don't try to remember individual pieces on individual squares; instead, they chunk the pieces into groups. So on the board here they would remember five chunks of information, each with several pieces in it.

2. This is combined with seeing patterns, which then make sense of these chunks. These use deeper understanding because they are invoking game strategies rather than superficial patterns of the pieces. This is all about making 'principled' sense of the information.

The importance of this is brought home when these same pieces are randomly shuffled on the board; grandmasters then remember only eight or so pieces. This is because, like novices, they have to fall back on to remembering individual pieces, as they cannot be organized into more powerful higher-order patterns.

We are capable of doing this ourselves. I can remember only a handful of letters from the chain

dckqsdxlasmxjdnijcbhks

but all of them from

jackandjillwentupthehill.

While I generally falter when remembering a shopping list, I have no difficulty remembering all the premier division football scores after just

41

one hearing. My bet would be that every reader has an area of memory that surprises friends and colleagues (who know of many memory lapses elsewhere). The point we return to in later chapters is that expert learning involves understanding the bigger picture in order to make sense of the detail, something often missing in the classroom.

Chess is a learned skill

This is obvious at one level; if we have never seen a chessboard, or its representation, we will be no good at chess. So opportunity is essential. However, there may still be a lurking assumption that you have to be a particular type of person to be a serious chess player – a similar assumption may hold for being a mathematician or musician. The evidence, as we shall see, makes this look unlikely. What is far more obvious is that grandmasters have had special opportunities, are highly motivated and put in their 10,000 hours of deliberate practice and more. These hours were not spent simply playing chess; grandmasters study chess through its rich history of games, gambits and moves. The phenomenal Polgar sisters are reckoned to have a library of over 10,000 chess books, which they have systematically studied (for more about the Polgar sisters, see the box below). This means that the grandmaster has a vast repertoire of knowledge and past experience on which to draw during a game. Like any expert, this level of organized experience allows them to recognize quickly what is happening and how best to deal with it.

The making of grandmasters – the Polgar sisters[58]

The three Hungarian Polgar sisters, Susan, Sofia and Judit, are among the most illustrious players in the history of chess. Susan

42

was the top-rated female player in the world at the age of 14 and the first woman player in history to become a grandmaster. Like many other female experts, obstacles were placed in her way; for example, even though she had qualified for the 1986 World Championship, she was not allowed to enter – it was for men only.

Her younger sister Sofia won the Hungarian under-11 championship for girls at age 5. As a 15-year-old she beat many of the world's greatest male players in a 1989 competition in Rome, where she secured eight consecutive victories, a performance rated as the all-time fifth best in the world.

Judit, the youngest sister, became the world's youngest grandmaster, male or female, at the age of 15 and was the top female player for over a decade.

What made the Polgar family remarkable?
No surprise that dedicated parents are at the heart of this amazing success story. Their father, Lazlo, was an educational psychologist who argued that talent was the result of hard work and that the educational system could be transformed if people recognized this. His ideas did not go down well in his local municipality, which he put down to people thinking that 'excellence is only open to others, not themselves'.

To make his point he decided to demonstrate his claims through his children. Although he was not a serious chess player, he decided this would be a good way to demonstrate his theory 'because it is objective'. People might have argued whether an artist or writer was world class, but in chess 'there is no possibility of argument'.

Lazlo read up on the pedagogy of chess and taught Susan at home, spending many hours a day on chess even before she was 4. His approach was jovial and he made much of the drama of the game. By her fifth birthday she was a chess enthusiast and won her first competition 10–0 against girls twice her age. The younger sisters did not start their training until later, though their father had encouraged them to handle and enjoy chess pieces from a much earlier age.

A feature of the training regime for the sisters is that they enjoyed it. The interaction with their father and his demands worked positively for them – 'We spent a lot of hours on the chessboard, but it did not seem like a chore because we loved it,' Judit has commented.

And the response?
As you might expect, many could not resist natural talent explanations. Having three top chess players in the same family suggested a family gift that, despite his claims about hard work and practice, produced the three most talented female chess players in history. When he was offered funding to adopt three boys from developing countries to see if this could be replicated, Lazlo was keen to accept. His wife Clara was not – she didn't have the energy for another experiment, especially as she thought 'the first time round would be enough to prove the theory'.

Lazlo's own verdict on the response is a telling one that resonates throughout this book: 'Maybe some people just do not want to believe in the power of practice.' Matthew Syed comments, 'Polgar's insights are repudiated by most academics and ignored by society. . . . the talent theory of expertise continues to reign supreme.'[59]

Studies of chess and chess players shaped some of the key discoveries about expertise, which have been confirmed and elaborated in many other activities. These can be grouped into four key findings:

1. Becoming an expert requires both opportunities and the motivation to succeed.

2. It involves extensive and long-term deliberate practice.

3. It requires extensive knowledge, which is organized through deep understanding so that more is remembered and relevant information can be readily accessed.

4. It includes reflection on thought processes and methods.

Expertise needs opportunity and motivation

People do not become experts by accident, though what they are experts in will often be determined by time and place. We are not surprised to find out that many of the key figures in the computer revolution were born within a couple of years of each other in America. We can do the same with art, music and sport in which there may have been 'golden ages' in particular countries ranging from art in fifteenth-century Florence to today's long-distance runners from East Africa.

As we have seen already, opportunity and support have often come from within the family. Earl Woods is playing golf with 2-year-old Tiger with his specially made clubs, the Williams sisters learn tennis because their father has noticed how much tennis players can earn, and the Polgar sisters learn chess because their father wants to demonstrate our capacity to learn. For others the spark has come from elsewhere. Here are two examples of schools and teachers providing it:

Bill Gates – right school, right time

Even when a particular local culture may provide the spark, some individuals stand out. Bill Gates came to dominate the computing world through Microsoft as a result of opportunities at his school. He had just moved to a well-heeled private school in Seattle in which the 'Mothers' club' raised money for various school causes. In 1968 they put $3000 into creating a computer room, unusual in itself at that time. More remarkable was that this contained a time-sharing terminal to a mainframe computer, when nearly all university and commercial programming was being done through slow and laborious batch-card systems. When this money ran out, one of the governors linked them with another company that needed its new computer programs checked, something the adolescent Gates and friends did at weekends and during the evenings. This company went bankrupt, but by then they had found another one that allowed them free computer time in exchange for developing software to automate company payrolls. Here they ran up thousands of hours of computing time, with Gates estimating that these 15–16-year-olds spent at least 20–30 hours a week programming. This came to a sticky end when Paul Allen, the co-founder of Microsoft, got them thrown out for stealing passwords and crashing the system. By then Allen had found a 24-hour computer terminal at the University of Washington that was free if you were prepared to use it in the early hours of the morning. Gates was, and as it was within walking distance of Gates's home, he would sneak out of his house between 3 and 6am in order to do this. (His mother later commented, 'We always wondered why it was so hard for him to get up in the morning.')

In line with this book's theme of 'multipliers', Gates then got further opportunities when he was contacted by a large power company desperate for programmers familiar with their software.

So the 18-year-old Gates asked his school to let him be absent for a term. The school agreed, treated this as his independent study project, a good example of a school being flexible enough to create opportunities.[60]

This account undermines the talent myth of Bill Gates as the Harvard student who had a bright idea while in his first year and then left to set up his company. Gates was given opportunities at school, which exposed him to state-of-the-art computing. These provided the spark and he was soon obsessed with computing and clocked up well over 10,000 hours of purposeful practice before he ever got to Harvard. It was his experience that provided the springboard for his innovations; he knew more than others and could harness this into powerful new applications.

Sir Steve Redgrave – what a difference a teacher makes
Steve Redgrave is Britain's greatest Olympian rower, with a tally of five gold medals spread over five Olympics. His route to rowing glory was an unlikely one. There was no history of rowing in the family, his father was an unassuming local builder, and he went to a local comprehensive school in an area where grammar schools creamed off those who passed the 11+ selection tests. This was in Marlowe, on the River Thames, where rowing was often the preserve of the privileged, including private and selective schools. However, at this school was an English teacher, Francis Smith, who coached the motley Marlowe High School rowing teams. His training methods were unorthodox – would he even be allowed to teach today? As part of fitness training he would bundle the team into his car at lunchtime, drive off and then tell them to get out and run back to school. The team would train on the river five or six days a week

with boats borrowed from the local rowing club, training he managed to make fun for the students.

The multipliers came when he entered them for competitions, winning at the very first attempt. This unorthodox rowing team went on to beat all the leading schools and by 1976 had won the under-16s national championship. What Redgrave calls 'this motley crew from the secondary modern[61] in our invisible string vests and knotted handkerchiefs' were up against 'smartly uniformed teams from private schools'. Uniquely, they even competed against the GB squad for a place in the 1979 World Championship. Redgrave sums up his teacher's contribution:

> without his own perseverance with a bunch of Secondary Modern kids I would never have stepped into a boat at all. And for that I will always be grateful.[62]

Expertise involves extensive and long-term deliberate practice

As mentioned earlier, Malcolm Gladwell popularized the idea that nobody becomes great without 10,000 hours of purposeful practice. This was not just a figure he plucked from the air; it is the best approximation from the expertise research. Much of the early research into chess players and musicians talked in terms of ten years of preparation before becoming a top performer. This approximates to about 1000 hours a year, an average of around three hours every day.

The pivotal study here was of musicians attending Berlin's elite Academy of Music in the early 1990s.[63] The students were divided into three groups: those judged to be future world-class soloists, those who would be likely to become professional musicians and those likely to become music teachers.

What was it that made the difference between the musicians in these three groups? The research investigated the background of the students: when did they start playing?, what teaching had they received?, how much had they practised? They found no systematic differences between the three groups regarding when they started playing (around age 5) or how much they practised early on. However, by age 8, differences began to emerge in the amount of practice, with the top-performing group averaging 16 hours a week at age 14 and over 30 hours a week of dedicated practice a week by age 20, far more than the other groups.

However, it is not just the time spent in practice that is important, but the deliberate and purposeful *quality* of the practice. The top musicians spent most of their hours in intensive individual practice and when elite players were studied, it was found that their practice was so intense, for example, concentrating on just one difficult page of music, that they would split it into two shorter sessions, typically one in the morning and one in the afternoon. What was also noticeable is that

> ❝It is not just the time spent in practice that is important, but the deliberate and purposeful *quality* of the practice.❞

they allowed themselves time to relax and recoup in between so that their lives 'were simultaneously more relaxed and more productive' than those who spread their work through the day 'never escaping a sense of stress and anxiety'.[64]

There is a temptation to dismiss the 10,000 hours claim on the grounds that '10,000 hours of piano practice wouldn't turn me into a concert pianist.' This is likely to be true if practice is simply seen as putting in the hours without a deep desire, and help, to constantly improve. Practice would be well within the comfort zone, for example, playing for pleasure what we can already play well. My tennis is like this – I practise shots that produce rallies that are pleasurable and I don't bother with serving because I'm no good at it and it spoils the fun. This is the antithesis of deliberate practice; if my serving is weak, I should practise it until it gets better, even if the process is painful and grim. Good coaches, though, can make it more pleasurable. Richard Williams invented all sorts of training games using traffic cones and anything else he could find in their impoverished neighbourhood so that his daughters Venus and Serena would practise for hours without feeling it was a chore.

Deliberate practice involves risk-taking

> "For those wanting to excel, *failure is an essential part of training*, from which we can often learn more than from routine success. Matthew Syed calls this the 'paradox of expert performance' – that 'excellence is about stepping outside the comfort zone . . . Progress is built, in effect, upon the foundations of necessary failure.'"

Having mastered so much, we might expect elite performers to stay within their large comfort zones when practising. This is not the case, since even in those sports where there is a strong risk of physical injury during practice, experts continue to take risks that others don't, in order to make the difficult more routine. The Japanese figure skater Shizuka Arakawa, winner of the gold medal in the 2006 Winter Olympics, had over many years perfected an 'impossible' move.[65] The practice for this and her other moves involved repeated falls and it was calculated that she had fallen at least 20,000 times in practice over the 19 years she had been skating. For those wanting to excel, *failure is an essential part of training*, from which we can often learn more than from routine success. Matthew Syed calls this the 'paradox of expert performance' – that 'excellence is about stepping outside the comfort zone . . . Progress is built, in effect, upon the foundations of necessary failure.'[66]

This has huge implications, as we see later, for how we think about risk-taking in learning.

Leaving the comfort zone

If we stay in our comfort zones, we may maintain our level of skill but we are unlikely to get any better. It is only when we move outside this into the *learning zone* that we make significant improvements. This is the zone in which we are being stretched to master new skills and knowledge. The skill of the teacher, as we shall see, is to move the learner into this zone. We can sometimes misjudge demands and push the learner into the *panic zone* where nothing is learned. Figure 2 illustrates these zones.

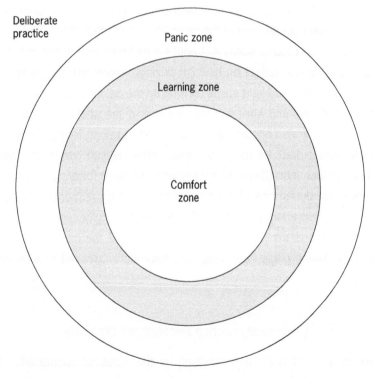

Figure 2 Deliberate practice
Source: Colvin, 2008

A good example of how this works is car driving. Most of us have done our 10,000 hours of driving, but few of us are experts. Why? Because our driving is overwhelmingly in the *comfort zone*, with attention focused on a radio programme, music or conversation. For those who drive to work there are often those moments when we are surprised to find we've arrived home – 'Oh, I'm home!' – because of an absorbing radio programme. My guess is that there has been little improvement in the last 5000 driving hours of our driving; indeed, the advent of such features as reversing sensors may mean our driving skills have actually diminished. This is because we move into the *learning zone* only when conditions are difficult or we have a new car with some unfamiliar controls – so I have to learn not to wash the windscreen every time I want to signal to turn. When I encounter bad weather or road conditions, I notice that I turn off my radio in order to concentrate and reflect on how I'm driving. I move into the *panic zone* when an unfamiliar red light starts blinking on the dashboard. In the learning zone I would stop and work out what it was and see what I could do about it; in the panic zone I become irrational and start talking to my car ('Please get me home; don't let me down now; come on, you can do it'). Some may remember John Cleese in the episode of *Fawlty Towers* where his car breaks down during one of his emergencies and his response is to open the bonnet, find a large branch and beat the car engine with it ('I warned you . . .'). This is a pure panic zone reaction. Like the comfort zone, no learning is taking place here: reactions have just regressed to a primitive stage.

Deliberate practice encourages creativity

There is a talent myth that creativity is the result of spontaneity. The implication is that intense practice will get in the way of this freedom to come up with new ideas. The evidence suggests the opposite. When scientists such as Einstein make their creative discoveries, these are invariably the result of intense study of the problem that has preoccupied them. Their insights come because they have mastered what is known and then go beyond this by reframing the problem. This does not mean that they have not had a 'eureka' moment in which the solution comes to them in a moment of illumination, but simply that it comes from deep absorption with a problem rather than a sudden out-of-the-blue idea. The same is the case with writers and artists: their most creative works come on the back of extensive practice. So, for example, behind the Brontë sisters' literary masterpieces lay years of creative writing as children in which they jointly created fantasy worlds and developed stories that laid the foundations for classics such as *Wuthering Heights*. In one 15-month period the young Brontës wrote 22 little books, averaging 80 pages each. These were highly derivative, drawing on magazines and other books, and very juvenile. Presentation was even worse: 'Their slapdash writing, appalling spelling, and non-existent punctuation [lasted] well into their late teenage years.'[67] One fascinating feature of their writing was that it was miniscule and done in tiny two-inch high books – so that it avoided adults' comments and censure since they could not read it. On her seventeenth birthday Charlotte's father gave her a notebook with the plea 'all that is written in this book, must be in a good, plain, legible hand'.

Expertise requires deep knowledge, with extensive memory and skills based on it

Organize knowledge better: remember more

By organizing their knowledge at a deeper, principled level, experts are able to handle more and see more. So chess masters can play games simultaneously and remember the moves in each one and, if they really want to show off, can play these games blindfold. London black cab taxi drivers have 'the knowledge' of London's roads, which means they do not need maps or satellite navigation systems, something that is certainly not true of London's mini-cab drivers. One of the key features of these highly developed *long-term working memories*[68] is that they are organized in a way that allows speedy retrieval, rather than the painfully slow ransacking of our memory banks that many of us go through when faced with a novel problem. This organization is at a deep level so that the evaluation of a situation would be in terms of key principles. For example, when novice physicists are compared with expert ones, novices organize the information around surface features, while experts recode them in terms of basic principles of physics. So a problem involving balancing a cart on an inclined plane is treated as a 'balance-of-forces' problem by experts, while for novices it will be viewed in terms of superficial features – a problem specific to carts and inclined planes.[69] What this also means is that for experts new problems are often minor variants of situations in which they know what principles to use, while for novices every new problem is a new problem: 'One becomes an expert by making routine what to the novice requires creative problem-solving.'[70]

See more

"The specialist can look at the same X-rays as other doctors and yet see more in them, picking up small yet significant diagnostic details."

Because of the way they organize their thinking, experts can often grasp the bigger picture more easily. This then allows them to focus on the key details, allowing them to pick up significant information that others might miss. This is at the heart of expert diagnosis in medicine; the specialist can look at the same

X-rays as other doctors and yet see more in them, picking up small yet significant diagnostic details.

There are similar findings with expert pilots and drivers. One of the developed abilities that distinguishes them from regular pilots and drivers is their *situation awareness*. Expert pilots:

- surprisingly perhaps, do *more* pre-flight preparation than their colleagues, focusing on planning and preparation for the flight, for example, checking conditions; this involves active interrogation of the information they have and, for military pilots, being more proactive during briefings;

- 'think ahead of the aircraft'; during a flight they are continually engaged in 'what if' thinking, so that they are ready if any of these situations materialize;

- have high levels of automatic skills that allow them to focus on key issues; inexperienced pilots were easily distracted and overwhelmed by the complex demands of flying;

- have well-developed mental models that allow them to evaluate situations rapidly both in relation to where they are and how they are flying.[71]

There have been very similar findings for expert drivers. These show better hazard awareness than less experienced drivers as a result of more effective scanning patterns and better search models. Like the expert pilots, expert drivers are more alert to hazards than inexperienced drivers. Having automated skills doesn't mean they drive in the comfort zone; rather, they free them up to operate more effectively in the learning zone: 'experienced drivers are conducting a more efficient and effective search for hazards rather than simply lowering their criterion for what constitutes a hazard'.[72]

Expertise involves reflection

All great artists and thinkers [are] great workers, indefatigable not only in inventing, but also in rejecting, sifting, transforming, ordering.

(Friedrich Nietzsche[73])

Experts constantly reflect on what and how they are doing, and it is often from this process that their creative contributions come. Charles Darwin reflected on his world-changing findings, and their implications for people's religious beliefs for over 20 years before publishing. For top sports stars the timing may be in seconds – what do I need to change about my game in order to deal with the way my opponent is playing, why is this shot not working? Making processes and skills automatic does not produce robots; it frees experts up to think more deeply about the really difficult areas. The discoveries of Marie Curie illustrate Nietzsche's claim well. Here was a scientist who was indeed indefatigable, often at a cost to her health, and who never stopped reflecting on what she was finding (see box below).

Marie Curie – a case study of creative and reflective expertise

Marie Curie was a remarkable scientist by any standards, the first woman to receive a doctorate in France, the first woman anywhere to earn a doctorate in physics, the first to be awarded a Nobel Prize for physics and the first person to be awarded a second Nobel Prize, this time in chemistry for the isolation of the elements radium and polonium.

Opportunities. Marie Curie had to create her own opportunities, given the odds were stacked against her; she was a Polish émigré who came to Paris to study because, as a woman, she could not go to university in Poland. She funded this by working as a governess in Poland for three years and then lived in poverty while a student in Paris. She seized every opportunity for study at the Sorbonne, coming top in her Master's courses in mathematics and physics.

Deliberate practice. It was her steely determination and scientific curiosity that led to her groundbreaking contributions. She became interested in the newly discovered radioactivity and chose this for her doctoral research. She spent four years, assisted by her husband Pierre Curie, in appalling conditions (a floorless and leaking wooden hut) sifting and distilling uranium waste they had begged from an Austrian glass factory until she isolated the new elements.

Knowledge base and creativity. Marie Curie mastered what was known about radioactivity and then hypothesized about the existence of new and far more radioactive elements. The idea of material generating, rather than just reflecting, energy upset the 'normal science' of the time and so ran into opposition. Her evidence proved convincing. Not satisfied with this she encouraged medical applications in the treatment of tumours.

Reflection. The discovery of radium was a classic example of reflecting on anomalies in what was known at the time. Why was radioactivity so uneven in its emission in the substances being studied? This could just have been treated as a given ('it just is') – but the expert scientist could not settle for this.

The Curies also thought deeply on the nature of science, reflections that led them to refuse to patent their discoveries, because they believed science should be for the benefit of all.

The message of this chapter is that to become a top performer in any field needs opportunities, motivation, good teaching and extensive purposeful practice. Expertise does not arrive by accident, nor is creativity an isolated spontaneous event – it invariably builds on mastery of skills and knowledge. The task now is to see how this translates to teaching and learning.

Questions for discussion

1. What would your response be to the questions 'What am I good at and how and why did I become good?' Discuss your responses with colleagues and look for commonalities.

2. How well do these align with the claims of this chapter?

3. What do you know about the development of one of your favourite experts/heroes and heroines?

4. What do you see as the implications of the expertise findings in this chapter for education?

3

Digging Deep: Expectations, Self-Belief and Challenge

Children develop only as the environment demands development.

(Sherman and Key[74])

Most students who become interested in an academic subject do so because they have met a teacher who was able to pique their interest.

(Mihalyi Csikszentmihalyi[75])

It is one thing to know how Marie Curie or Tiger Woods got to develop their expertise, another to get a class of 30 pupils to learn on a wet Friday afternoon. The next three chapters seek to bridge this chasm by applying to the classroom what we have learned about ability and expertise. The 'expert learner' here is ambiguous – we want our students to become expert learners but to do this we need to learn to be expert teachers ourselves. I see this expertise as having much in common with expertise in other professional domains, particularly clinical and coaching ones.

I've used 'digging deep' because a regular and haunting refrain from athletes at the 2012 Olympics was, 'I had to dig deep.' These were the

> "A regular and haunting refrain from athletes at the 2012 Olympics was, 'I had to dig deep.' These were the situations in which they needed to call on all their training, experience, knowledge and self-belief to provide the marginal difference between winning and losing."

situations in which they needed to call on all their training, experience, knowledge and self-belief to provide the marginal difference between winning and losing. When David Weir, born disabled and raised on a tough housing estate, won his fourth gold medal in the wheelchair (T54) Paralympic marathon, having already won the 800, 1500 and 5000 metre titles that same week, he commented that he had had to 'dig very deep' for the final sprint. That he even had the strength to speak was remarkable, as he then thanked all those who had supported him through his thousands of hours of practice that had led up to this. Here I use 'digging deep' to capture both the effort needed and the quality of learning to be achieved.

The key findings from the previous chapters are as follows. Expertise:

- is learned, not inherited;
- involves high expectations and clear goals;
- requires strong motivation and resilience;
- uses powerful mental frameworks;
- needs extensive deliberate practice;
- incorporates skilled diagnostics and feedback.

In this chapter I focus largely on the first four of these and examine educational expectations, how learners see themselves, and the importance of motivation. One of the key features of expertise is that experts develop a mental model with which to organize both understanding and memory. This allows them to see the big picture, spot patterns and identify the unusual. It also makes possible the 'chunking' of large amounts of information as they absorb it into their framework. So, while the chess grandmaster can look at a game of chess for a few seconds and remember where all the pieces are on the board, the novice can remember only a few individual pieces.

So what steps have to be taken to move classroom learning closer to expert learning? In this chapter we look at four steps that may help close the gap:

1. Raise expectations by shifting away from fixed ability labels to an incremental view of learning.
2. Expect more of our students, particularly the relatively disadvantaged.
3. Encourage deep learning approaches.
4. Find ways to motivate learners, particularly those with little appetite for education.

Step 1. Watch our language – move away from fixed ability talk

The first step to bridging the gap between experts and Friday's class is to recognize they are the same species. The gifted are not a separate, and differently endowed, breed. The difference is in the way abilities have been *developed* and central to this are opportunities, support and motivation. The danger is in assuming a 'low ability class' is a lost cause because nature has dealt them a weak hand. This is what Binet challenged over a century ago, the 'brutal pessimism' of Anglo-Saxon thinking.

Yet messages *are* sent that children attribute to personal limitations rather than other causes. In schools where children walk about with 'I am gifted and talented' badges (yes, there are such schools), what are the other students to think?

What message does being in the bottom stream for maths send? The message may be 'I'm no good at maths' and this may quickly slide into the learned helplessness of 'so there's no point in trying'. Maths is a good example of how British culture plays into this, the belief that some people can do maths and others can't, with many adults treating innumeracy as a 'badge of honour'.[76] Jo Boaler reports that 88 per cent of children placed in ability groups at age 4 remain in the same groupings until they leave school. She adds:

> 66That 88 per cent of children placed in ability groups at age four remain in the same groupings until they leave school . . . is one of the most chilling statistics I have ever read . . . For schools to decide what children can do, for the rest of their school career, when they are four years old – or any other primary school age – is nothing short of criminal.99– Jo Boaler

This is one of the most chilling statistics I have ever read . . . For schools to decide what children can do, for the rest of their school career, when they are four years old – or any other primary school age – is nothing short of criminal.[77]

So what do we make of this statement from England's Education Secretary?

Children from wealthy backgrounds of low cognitive ability overtake children from poor backgrounds and high cognitive ability before they even arrive at school . . . So, in effect rich thick kids do better than poor clever children, and when they arrive at school the situation gets worse. (Michael Gove, Education Secretary, 2010)[78]

So we are born 'thick' or 'clever', though the environment then makes a difference. To his credit, Michael Gove recognizes the role of the environment and that, with the opportunities rich kids get, much can be achieved. However, as we saw in Chapter 2, this is still simplistic thinking, awarding a label for life within the first two years. I return to the example of language development: we are born with a genetic capacity for language, yet it is our interaction with the environment that determines the language we speak and how well we do this. This is relevant to Gove's claim because we know that there are massive class differences in language development and language plays a key role in the measurement of intelligence and in academic achievement.

The classic research here was by the American psychologists Betty Hart and Todd Risley who were investigating why poor children fell behind in their mental development well before they reached school. They followed 42 families from three socioeconomic levels for three years, sampling the number of words spoken to the young children. The contrasts were dramatic:

- Children from professional homes were, on average, exposed to 1500 more spoken words per hour (2,153 to 616 words) than children in welfare homes, a total of eight million per year.

- In the first four years a child from a professional background received over half a million more instances of encouraging feedback to discouraging feedback (a six-to-one ratio), for a working-class child, it was 100,000 (two-to-one) while the welfare child received 125,000 more discouragements than encouragements (one positive to two negatives – 5-to-11 per hour).[79]

The temptation is to dismiss this as something that wouldn't happen in our classrooms. We have seen that experts reflect continuously on their practice and a constructive first move would be to monitor the language we use with our students. Does our language change when we work with lower-attaining students? Are we more directive with them? With whom do

> "Does our language change when we work with lower-attaining students? Are we more directive with them? With whom do we do most joking? Does the language of feedback change in relation to achievement?"

we do most joking? Does the language of feedback change in relation to achievement?[80]

Switch to progression talk

A change of vocabulary would help here. We need terms that signal where someone is in their learning progression rather than their mental status ('low ability'). The traditional language of apprenticeship may be a useful alternative, with progression in learning placed on a continuum.[81] For present purposes the key steps are *naive, novice, apprentice, expert*, though we will need to subdivide some of these. *Naive* is the stage at which virtually nothing is known about a particular subject or topic. So, for example, children at the naive stage in science might believe that the sun orbits the earth, a belief with a long pedigree, or that the earth goes round the sun once a day. Similarly, the phases of the moon may be put down to clouds, or shadows cast by planets or the sun or the earth.[82] By the *novice* phase there will have been some exposure to the domain, but novices make only limited connections between pieces of information or skills. So the student now knows the earth rotates around the sun and spins on its axis but may struggle to combine this information when asked about eclipses and seasons. By the *apprenticeship* stage there has

> "The expert is the *meaningful learner* who has made sense of the particular domain, who can see the connections and transfer understandings to new problems."

been more exposure to the subject or skill, there is a more complex understanding and the learner is beginning to think like a historian or scientist. At the end of this stage the apprentice will be proficient and begin to work without continuous supervision, traditionally the 'journeyman' who can perform a day's labour unsupervised. The key transition here is from 'learning music' to 'becoming a musician'.[83]

The expert is the *meaningful learner* who has made sense of the particular domain, who can see the connections and transfer understandings to new problems.

Step 2. Raise expectations

However, if the environment makes a critical difference, how are we to take Michael Gove's 'and when they arrive at school the situation gets worse'? This is not just political rhetoric; the findings come from the 1970 British Birth Cohort Study, which followed over 7000 children, born in the same week, into adulthood. What this showed was that children from low socioeconomic status (SES) backgrounds whose test scores were in the top quarter at 22 months showed a steady relative decline in scores up to age 10, while children from high SES families who scored in the bottom quarter made steady progress up to age 10.[84] This is obviously about much more than just schooling – but what happens in the classroom must contribute. Are relatively different expectations placed on children from low SES backgrounds?

Further evidence for this comes from research on 15-year-olds from 23 countries who took the 2009 PISA reading tests.[85] This showed that the average reading age gap in England between children from professional and working-class homes was 2.5 years, larger than 19 other countries, and twice the gap in Germany, Finland and Iceland. So something is going on in societies that produce such gaps, with Scotland, the USA and New Zealand having even greater ones. These data also show that while England has steadily improved the performance of those low SES students in 'the long tail of underachievement', it has not done the same for higher achieving low SES students relative to their more affluent peers.

Sending messages

A knee-jerk response may be to look at conditions in schools, for example, class-size and the state of the buildings, but I do not think this line of argument can be sustained, especially as other countries operate with larger classes and worse buildings. It seems more likely that this is about the social expectations about education that parents, children and teachers carry. 'Fixed ability' thinking may play a big part in this, especially if children decide that education is for others, not for them, and they don't have what it takes. This message was quite clear with 11+ selection tests, but is still there with test scores, streaming and ability group teaching. So while most children in England do not take the 11+, they will take the Cognitive Abilities Test (CATs) on entry to secondary school, the results of which are often treated as measures of fixed ability (see p.10).

What we have learned from the study of expertise is that ability develops and is malleable. A key factor is that of *expectation*, those who excel want to and are encouraged to believe they can excel. So the children of professional parents are expected to achieve at school, especially if the parents are paying the school in order for their offspring to do well.

The problem for the wet Friday class is that some students may be harbouring more negative expectations, the 'learned helplessness' that they are no good at school stuff. The role of ability labels and of the public grading of achievement is often underestimated in this process.

Learned helplessness: Hannah the nothing

Hannah is the name given to an 11-year-old pupil in England in a class studied by Diane Reay and Dylan Wiliam.[86] This class was being prepared for the national tests (SATs) that children take in the last year of junior school in England. These tests carry no major selection consequences for the pupils, since their secondary schools would already have been chosen, but the results are critically important for their schools and teachers, as they are judged by them. The task is to get as many children as possible to attain level 4 and above,[87] as school and national targets are based on this. As a result of the testing and drilling, children become well aware of their expected level. It is in this context that the following exchange took place:

HANNAH: I'm really scared about the SATs. Mrs O'Brien [a teacher at the school] came in and talked to us about our spelling and I'm no good at spelling and David [the class teacher] is giving us times tables tests every morning and I'm hopeless at times tables so I'm frightened I'll do the SATs and I'll be a nothing.

DIANE: I don't understand, Hannah. You can't be a nothing.

HANNAH: Yes, you can 'cos you have to get a level like a level 4 or level 5 and if you're no good at spellings and times tables you don't get those levels and so you're a nothing.

DIANE: I'm sure that's not right.

HANNAH: Yes it is 'cos that's what Mrs O'Brien was saying.

To make this claim of nothingness even more poignant, the authors point out that Hannah was 'an accomplished writer, a gifted dancer and artist and good at problem solving, yet none of those skills make her somebody in her own eyes. Instead, she constructs herself as a failure, an academic non-person.'

Hannah's responses are indicative of the identities learners take on in school. I'm sure her teachers would be horrified to find their comments had been interpreted this way, but through the pupils' eyes this was the message they were getting. Tamara Bibby has also found very similar attitudes in her research on the primary classroom:

> Children start to think of themselves as levels. And it's wrapped up with morality and goodness. Good people work hard and listen in class. If it suddenly becomes clear your mate gets lower levels than you, are they a good person? It can put real pressure on a friendship.[88]

Whatever language we choose to describe students, the focus should be on their *progression in learning* rather than on ability labels that shape what the students think they are capable of doing, as in the case of 'I'll be a Nothing' Hannah. We are going to find it difficult to motivate learners to take on demanding goals if labels and groupings suggest these are not for the likes of them. So, if we are to progress their learning, the wet Friday group is better viewed as reluctant novices rather than as low ability no-hopers.

How can we best develop a 'can do' culture in teaching and learning? One move may be to focus on learning demands rather than grades, marks or levels.

Step 3. Make deep demands

What is the biggest difference between expert and experienced teachers? When John Hattie and his team researched this question, they found differences on five main dimensions, but by far the most significant one was that *they set more challenging tasks*. Hattie found that 74 per cent of the work from classes of expert teachers was judged to reflect a deep level of understanding, compared with 29 per cent of work samples from experienced teachers. As a consequence they also found differences in the depth at which students learned to process information:

> Students who are taught by expert teachers exhibit an understanding of the concepts targeted in the instruction that is more coherent and at a higher level of abstraction than the understanding achieved by students in classes taught by experienced, but not expert, teachers.[89]

We know that experts develop powerful mental frameworks that allow them to organize their approaches to a task. These are at a 'principled' level, so expert scientists look for scientific principles with which to solve a problem while novices will be drawn towards the surface features. The same applies to teaching, so how do we organize our approach so that we make deeper demands?

Surface, strategic and deep[90]

A classification that I have found useful in addressing the kind of learning that expertise involves is that of surface, strategic and deep learning approaches. It was developed with university students and based on the assumption that approaches to learning change over the degree course as specialism increases. The three approaches are summarized below. These are approaches to learning rather than personal dispositions, though the risk is that they easily slip into a label ('he's a surface learner'). I see expert learning as using a mix of strategic and deep learning approaches, the strategic encouraging organized study and self-monitoring, the deep approach leading to effective mental frameworks and improved understanding as learners 'make sense' of a domain.

Approaches to learning and studying[91]

Approach	Defining features
Surface	
Reproducing	Treating the course as unrelated bits of knowledge
Intention: to cope with course requirements	Memorizing facts and carrying out procedures routinely
	Finding difficulty in making sense of new ideas
	Seeing little value or meaning in either courses or tasks set
	Studying without reflecting on either purpose or strategy
	Feeling undue pressure and worry about work
Strategic	
Reflective organizing	
Intention: to achieve the highest possible grades	Putting consistent effort into studying
	Managing time and effort effectively
	Finding the right conditions and materials for studying
	Monitoring the effectiveness of ways of studying
	Being alert to assessment requirements and criteria
	Gearing work to the perceived preferences of lecturers
Deep	
Seeking meaning	Relating ideas to previous knowledge and experience
Intention: to develop ideas for yourself	Looking for patterns and underlying principles
	Checking evidence and relating it to conclusions
	Examining logic and argument cautiously and critically
	Being aware of understanding developing while learning
	Becoming actively interested in course content

So the surface approach leads to students asking what they need to do to get through, it's how to cobble together the necessary pass mark, something that encourages 'when you see that – do this . . .' teaching to the test. Understanding hardly comes into play; the learning isn't important.

The strategic approach, used by students who want to do well and get good grades, will be very familiar. These students are motivated and are learning to organize themselves for effective study. The issue is whether what is learned for a particular assessment is carried forward and integrated into a wider competency. This is where the familiar, and historical, complaints of employers come from, that students who have been successful in examinations cannot apply this in real life. Here is the interesting case study of Ruth Borland, who was the top student and scored maximum marks in Ireland's Leaving Certificate, the examination that is the passport to university. In an interview with the *Irish Times* she was asked the secret of her success. Here it is:

> Learning the formula for each exam and practising it endlessly. I got an A1 in English because I knew exactly what was required in each question. I learned off the sample answers provided by the examiners and I knew how much information was required and in what format in every section of the paper. That's how you do well in these examinations . . . There's no point in knowing about stuff that is not going to come up in the exams. I was always frustrated by teachers who would say 'You don't need to know this for the exams but I'll tell you anyway.' I wanted my A1 – what's the point of learning material that won't come up in the exams?[92]

Do we applaud Ruth or are we dismayed by her highly strategic attitude? The postbag of the *Irish Times* cut both ways: those who were horrified to find one of the country's 'highest achievers to be so brutally dismissive of a broad view of learning' while others supported her determination. Ruth's response was that any criticism should be directed at the system itself:

> I chose not to fight the system but to play with it. I did what I had to do to achieve my goals; I played the game, if you will. I would not call this attitude 'utilitarian' but realistic. I got into college to study the courses I enjoy. I will have 'the pleasure of discovery' in business and economics courses.

Part of this game was to switch in her optional subjects to the business suite of subjects, her 'strong suit . . . for getting the points I needed', even though this meant changing schools. That business subjects were seen as an easier option was also the system's problem.

I suspect we all have a sneaking respect for this kind of focused determination, yet would want a bit more depth from such a capable student. We certainly don't need to pity Ruth – she was subsequently given an occasional column on the *Irish Times* to offer hints on exam preparation. I would treat Ruth at that stage as a *proficient apprentice* rather than an expert learner. She does what she needs to do and does it extremely well, but her focus is on what the examiners want rather than 'making sense' of it for herself and developing her own mental framework, key features of a deep learning approach and of expertise. Your response may be 'but that's how you get through exams' and, in a climate where good grades are critical for both student and teacher, I don't want to be too other-worldly. However, it is not the only route to good grades and encouraging a deeper approach may be more rewarding in both the short and long term.

Exam preparation – digging deeper

Paul Ayres and colleagues identified 25 exceptional teachers in terms of their success with students in the New South Wales high-stakes leaving examination. The criteria were that their results were in the top 1 per cent nationally for the previous six years and the students' results were better in the teacher's subject than in their other subjects (an ingenious part of the research design as it meant it wasn't just a case of always having the highest-performing students). The schools were representative in terms of socioeconomic status. What the researchers found through observation and interview was that these teachers did *not* take a strictly strategic approach; for example, they often chose more difficult options, because they thought they were more interesting, and were quite prepared to go beyond the syllabus if it deepened understanding. The researchers also found that these teachers, 17 of them female, were experienced, with an average age of 44, worked in close teams and stable faculties, and had a passion for their subject. Like the expert pilots of Chapter 2, they emphasized the importance of planning as a key part of their success. They saw class time as precious and allowed little or no 'dead time'. Their focus was on getting their students to think:

> While teachers used a wide range of teaching strategies to build student understanding, a key common factor was an emphasis on having students think, solve problems and apply knowledge. Simply reporting back knowledge or practising formulae outside the context of application was unusual. These teachers strongly saw their role in the classroom as challenging students, rather than 'spoon-feeding' information. They demonstrated ways of building notes and assisted in this process, but were never observed dictating a complete set of notes or having students simply copy notes without a context developed or a lead-up involving student responses.

These expert teachers also invested in oral work and group work, something often minimized in exam preparation classes:

While questioning in the whole-class situation was dominated by closed questions, this contrasted to the strategies teachers used when having students work alone or in groups. In fact, group work was more prominent than might have been expected in [exam] classes and was used for a variety of reasons, particularly activities oriented towards problem-solving. The closed questions that teachers used in the whole-class situation tended to be used to carefully build understanding of the material in layers and to make links to other aspects of the content. In effect, it served to both look back and look forward in the subject.[93]

> "Experts take risks in their practice. For teachers, risk-taking may involve going beyond the conventional routines of test preparation to ensure a deeper understanding of the domain by their students."

Experts take risks in their practice. For teachers, risk-taking may involve going beyond the conventional routines of test preparation to ensure a deeper understanding of the domain by their students. When an unexpected question pops up, and there may be more of these in examinations in England if Michael Gove has his way, the 'drilled' learner may have to deal with an unknown situation. For the 'principled' learner it may only be a variation on a theme.

Step 4. Motivate – the hardest step?

Looking around a wet Friday afternoon class is a reminder that the key problem is not the capacity to learn but the willingness. Mihalyi Csikszentmihalyi, one of the world's leading experts on student motivation, observes:

The chief impediments to learning are not cognitive. It is not that students cannot learn; it is that they do not wish to. If educators invested a fraction of the energy they now spend on trying to transmit information in trying to stimulate students' enjoyment of learning, we could achieve much better results.[94]

But how? In his *Talented Teenagers* Csikszentmihalyi and colleagues intensively followed the progress

> "The chief impediments to learning are not cognitive. It is not that students cannot learn; it is that they do not wish to." – Mihalyi Csikszentmihalyi

of top-achieving students, buzzing them on pagers at regular intervals, including outside school, at which point they would note down their activities and attitudes.[75] These records were analysed and showed that secondary school students were most motivated by the following:

- *When their teachers were personally involved in the subject and communicated this passion.* This echoes the apprenticeship model: the master had to be a practising expert. These students were very critical of, and switched off by, teachers who just went through the motions or were not personally involved in their subject.

- *When their teachers centred attention on challenges and the satisfaction of learning something new.* These teachers minimized 'the insidious impact of extrinsic pressures like competition, grades, needless rules and bureaucratic procedures' (p.191).

- *When their teachers provided informative activity-focused feedback* rather than the 'controlling' extrinsic feedback of rewards and punishment.

- *When their teachers had a flexible and dynamic attentional style* that involved skilled interaction with students and sought to match skills to challenges.

- *When their teachers allowed students freedom and autonomy to develop their own solutions and approaches.* While we might expect this in English and art, this response came through strongly from the mathematics and science students, for whom the pleasure was in finding their *own* solutions to a problem rather than learning a textbook method.

Motivating the academically unmotivated[95]

Csikszentmihalyi's findings were based on exceptional students, though they apply to many more.

However, most classes will have some students who have little personal interest, who may place limited value on what is being learned, and have limited confidence in whether they can achieve what is required. The task is then to generate *situational interest* that motivates. John Dewey introduced the idea of 'catch' and 'hold' over a century ago. Catching interest is what we are trying to do with Friday afternoon discussions, quizzes and computer activities; the dilemma is that they rarely lead to sustained interest. It is the 'hold' factors of meaningfulness and personal relevance that sustain. The expert teacher's skill is in finding materials or activities that can do both. Most experienced teachers of English will use novels and poems that they know will grab the class, even on a Friday, though these may not be prescribed texts – but experts will take risks here. Similarly, in science there may be demonstrations or problems that will puzzle students enough to catch them. Giving a compass to the young Albert Einstein was enough to arouse his curiosity – why did the needle behave as it did?

We know from research some of the factors that can help to stimulate situational interest. These will come as little surprise to expert teachers who will apply them routinely:

1. *Working with peers on learning tasks.* This is widely known and equally widely ignored. From interviews with sixty-five 16- and 17-year-old

'disengaged and disaffected' students in England Jacky Lumby found consistent messages that one of the four key factors that helped them in their learning was *social learning*, "cos if you are working with other people, if you get stuck on the question, then, and then they know it, then they can help you out and you are not asking the teacher all the time'.[96] This mirrors my own survey work with 13- to 14-year-old students as part of an evaluation of a national strategy pilot,[97] as do the other three factors of clarity of instruction, experiential learning ('activities, not writing') and clear direction on improvement. Is the problem here that we find it hard to cope with the thought that our students will at times learn better without us? This was what teachers in Black and Wiliam's action research on implementing assessment for learning found. They reported that the hardest professional shift was in doing less talking and letting students work together more.[98]

2. *Giving students choices increases involvement.* These choices do not have to be major ones, even quite trivial ones – 'choose one of these two problems' – may increase motivation simply because the student has made some sort of investment. This is a major theme in Daniel Pink's *Drive*, a bestseller that looks at motivation in business. His big idea is that we need to move from carrot-and-stick attempts to motivate to giving people more autonomy over how they conduct their work, so that motivation becomes more intrinsic. He argues that even for routine tasks we can improve motivation by:

> "Is the problem here that we find it hard to cope with the thought that our students will at times learn better without us?"

*   offering a rationale for why the task is necessary;
*   acknowledging that the task might be boring ('an act of empathy');

- allowing people to complete the task in their own way. 'Think autonomy, not control. State the outcome you need. But instead of specifying precisely the way to reach it . . . give them freedom over how they do the job.'[99]

3. *External incentives may help but have to be used with care.* To interest the less motivated we may need to offer some external incentives, particularly in the 'catch' phase. For many schools this may involve targets and tracking that are used to monitor progress; in others, stars and smiley faces are the currency. We know these work best when they are used in terms of the students' progress relative to their earlier work, rather than in comparison with others. Care is needed when the student begins to develop an intrinsic interest in the subject, since there is plenty of evidence that external rewards and incentives can undermine this fledgling interest.[100] This is also true for those students whose motivation comes from solving problems for themselves.

4. *Personal bests.* A familiar sight from the 2012 Olympics was 'PB' on the scoreboard, athletes who may not have won a medal but had recorded their best ever time, a source of great satisfaction on such a big stage. Andrew Martin has observed that 'personal best' is a routinely invoked concept in sporting contexts that 'receives surprisingly little attention in the educational domain'.[101] The motivational appeal of personal bests is that individuals are comparing their performances with what they have already achieved, so they are about attainable improvement. Martin's analysis suggests that personal bests are most effective when the tasks or goals are:

   a. *specific*, 'with clear information about what they are trying to achieve in the immediate future';

b. *challenging* in a way that gives a reason for wanting to achieve a particular outcome;

c. *competitively self-referenced* so that the individual is competing against her own previous performance rather than against that of others;

d. *focused on self-improvement* that builds on previous levels of performance.

> "The motivational appeal of personal bests is that individuals are comparing their performances with what they have already achieved, so they are about attainable improvement."

We know that people become experts as a result of placing high demands on themselves and being motivated to reach these goals. In the classroom this translates to high expectations and deeper approaches to learning. At the same time it involves more learner autonomy – we cannot spoon-feed deep learning. The next chapter looks in more detail at how we can help students have a clear understanding of where they are trying to get to in their learning.

Questions for discussion

1. How can you further develop the *progression talk* you use? Is the apprenticeship model useful? How useful or relevant are 'personal bests' in this respect?

2. How are your students encouraged to believe they can achieve?

3. How are deep learning demands placed on all your students – or are they restricted only to the high achievers?

4. What would be your own trusted 'catch and hold' lesson? Why does it work?

5. For a provocative account of how disadvantaged children can learn far more than we would expect, watch Sugata Mitra's *Hole in the Wall Project* on http://www.youtube.com/watch?v=dk60sYrU2RU (17 min. [accessed 2 Aug. 2013]). What is your response to this?

4

Is Everybody Clear?

You haven't taught until they have learned.

(John Wooden)

It's not that I haven't learned much. It's just that I don't understand what I'm doing.

(15-year-old[102])

John Wooden is a legendary American college basketball coach, a former top player who repeatedly coached teams to every honour in the book. The quote was a response to a colleague who complained that he had 'taught' his team a move but they 'just don't learn'. Wooden's response was that the problem was the teaching, not the students. His own coaching methods involved meticulous planning and analysis; his preparation for his *whole-part* method took as long as the practices themselves.

Whole-part coaching

In line with the expertise model I am using, Wooden believed that the players should first understand the whole concept of a particular play or strategy.

Having *explained*, he would *demonstrate* the whole move before breaking it down into its parts. These demonstrations were so thorough that 'they seemed, at the time, to be overkill . . . but he seldom had to explain something twice'.[103] Having understood the 'big picture', the next steps were *imitation* and *correction*, in which he broke down the moves and had the players copy them. A feature of his coaching was the way he provided intense on-the-spot feedback until the players mastered their moves. These were overwhelmingly *information-rich* comments on how to do it properly. He rarely criticized players for errors or used praise or blame, but neither did he leave it at the familiar 'you're-almost-there-so-here's-the-answer'. For him this 'nearly there' meant giving up on further analysis of student misunderstandings that would allow them to get it exactly right. The final step was *repetition*: the intention here is to repeat the desired performance until it becomes automatic, performing an operation until there is no conscious thought of the body movements needed. And 'the more the student does it correctly, the more the teacher backs off and allows him gradually to become independent'.[104]

The classroom isn't a basketball court and the skills we are trying to cultivate may be less tangible, but there are still some powerful messages here. In this chapter I recast them in terms of the more familiar language of learning intentions and success criteria, modelling and exemplars. I also introduce the idea of *mindful*, as opposed to mindless, repetition, and suggest we often underplay this in our teaching. At the heart of all this is *clarity*, with both teachers and students knowing what is being learned and why. John Hattie calls this 'visible teaching' in which 'teaching becomes visible to the student, and . . . the learning is visible to the teacher'.[105]

Clarifying the learning we want

Thinking is much more fun than memorizing

(Susan Brookhart[106])

I have yet to find a country that is not using an idealistic policy rhetoric about the 'twenty-first-century learner' required by the global knowledge economy. This learner is highly literate and numerate and is flexible, resourceful and able to learn for themselves as well as working well in groups to solve problems. Here's a dose of PISA[107] rhetoric:

> Are students prepared for future challenges? Can they analyse, reason and communicate effectively? Do they have the capacity to continue learning throughout life?[108]

Yet the educational policies introduced to achieve this vision generally encourage a very different approach to learning. The emphasis in many countries is on test and examination results and on accountability targets, with the result that learning is often reduced to preparation for tests. This kind of instrumental learning, highly teacher-dependent and test-geared, does not fit at all comfortably with the twenty-first-century lifelong learning rhetoric.[109] As teachers we are easily sucked into this, especially if performance pay is related to results. This is not to say that good results are not important – they are – but there are other ways to get them (see pp. 72–4). Here's a response to the PISA aspiration in which teaching to the test meant students were able to pass the high-stakes Texas Assessment of Academic Skills, even though the students had never learned the concepts on which they are being tested:

> As teachers become adept at this process, they can even teach students to answer correctly test items *intended* to measure students' ability to apply, analyze or synthesize, even though the students have not developed application, analysis or synthesis skills.[110]

❝Instrumental learning, highly teacher-dependent and test-geared, does not fit at all comfortably with the twenty-first-century lifelong learning rhetoric.❞

Expert learning has to go well beyond this. Michael Eraut defines learning as *a significant change in capability or understanding* from which he excludes 'the acquisition of further information when it does not contribute to such changes'.[111] I like this definition because it makes clear that new learning makes a difference to how we think or perform from then onwards – it leads to permanent capacity change.[112] So when we learn to swim or ride a bicycle, we have capacity change. I may not ride a bike for the next ten years but it would only take a wobbly couple of minutes before I was riding again. When I memorize a *Trivial Pursuits* answer for next time ('the golf tee'), this does not change capacity – it does not alter how I think or reason. The surface/strategic/deep distinctions of Chapter 3 may give us enough to work with, so that we can ask ourselves what kind of learning does this question or assignment require? There are other more detailed taxonomies that may offer more precision. Many will be familiar with Bloom's taxonomy,[113] though my own 'best buy' would be the SOLO taxonomy originally developed in schools by John Biggs and Kevin Collis, but now taken up by higher education.[114]

Going SOLO

Conceptually this taxonomy is extremely powerful, though some of its terminology can be daunting. For example, SOLO stands for Structure of the Observed Learning Outcomes, an accurate but clumsy description of SOLO's focus on *judging the quality of students' thinking from their work*. This taxonomy was based on analysing the work (the learning outcomes) of students and classifying it into five levels according to how information was linked and structured.

At this point the SOLO taxonomy may look less than exciting. What gives it its dynamism is what goes on within these classifications, particularly in the language associated with each level and the way in which our teaching and assessments have to be fit for purpose – what Biggs calls *constructive*

The SOLO taxonomy

Level	Features	Example
Prestructural	The information has no organization/is wrong	Cod is what people pray to
Unistructural	One relevant idea	Cod is an important food
Multistructural	Several strands of information but misses the relationship between them and to the whole	Cod is an important food, a species at risk and lives in colder seas
Relational	Links and integrates information to provide a coherent understanding of the whole	Because it's an important food source and is found near highly populated countries, cod is at risk from overfishing
Extended abstract	students begin to rethink their relational understanding, beginning to look at it differently, to generalize and to form hypotheses	The need for sustainable fishing policies, the ethical and economic implications of overfishing

alignment. This is another case of 'watch your language', especially the verbs we use. When we ask students to *name* or *identify*, this encourages unistructural outputs, necessary at the start of mastering something new. Verbs such as *combine, describe, list* require several independent aspects and reflect the multistructural level. Relational-level working is encouraged by verbs such as *analyse, compare and contrast, criticize, explain causes and justify,* which help to integrate information into a structure. The extended abstract will use verbs such *create, formulate, reflect* and *hypothesize* in order to generalize understanding to new domains. This again may seem self-evident, but John Biggs's research suggests that in practice we say we are demanding work at one level, but our verbs give us away. This is particularly true with tests and examinations that, despite course intentions to compare or to create, can easily fall back into recalling content at pre-relational levels. This is the basis of constructive alignment: How do we make sure there is a coherent match between learning intentions, student activity, teaching and assessment? Biggs and Tang see it as three stages:

1. Describe the *intended learning outcome* in the form of a verb (learning activity), its object (content) and specify the context and standard required.

2. Create a learning environment using *teaching/learning activities* that address that verb and therefore are likely to bring about the intended outcome.

3. Use *assessment tasks* that also contain that verb.[115]

This may seem obvious – but check the aims of your particular curriculum with its content and its assessment. The philosopher John White has provided a fascinating account of this in the National Curriculum in England, showing how the learning aims of the National Curriculum, which were not even formulated for the earlier versions, bore little relation to the content, with some of the curriculum developers admitting they did not even look at the aims until afterwards.[116] Assessment would then focus on the curriculum content, often undermining the aims by emphasizing recall rather than thinking.

Experts' learning – it's not just what you know but how you know it

We have seen how experts create a mental framework that allows them to hold and to access more information than others. So grandmasters can instantly make sense of a game of chess and expert scientists will view information at the level of principles. In teaching we both have to know about what we are teaching and be able to communicate this to our students. Lee Shulman has called this *pedagogical content knowledge* (PCK), which:

> represents the blending of content and pedagogy into an understanding of how particular topics, problems, or issues are organized, represented, and adapted to the diverse interests and abilities of learners, and presented for instruction.[117]

John Hattie has taken this a step further in suggesting there isn't a lot of difference between experienced and expert teachers in terms of *what* they know; the difference is in *how* they organize and use this knowledge. So expert teachers:

- have more integrated knowledge and can link new subject knowledge to students' prior knowledge and current lessons to other ones;
- can detect and use information that has most relevance and offer a wider range of strategies that students might use;
- adapt lessons (change, combine, add) according to students' needs;
- monitor learning and provide feedback;
- check and test out their hypotheses and seek negative evidence about their impact.[118]

This adaptive expertise is similar to that found in top coaches. What these coaches also have is a clear sense of progression in mastering the particular sporting skill. This is more difficult, but still essential, in school. In her 'Knowing what to do next: the hard part of formative assessment?'[119]

Margaret Heritage has shown how teachers are often accurate in diagnosing where learners are in their learning; the problem comes with what to do about it. Her analysis is that this is often the result of teachers not having a clear idea of *learning progression* and of the tasks, activities, interactions and tools that would encourage progression. So what is progression, for example, in history? What would we expect from children at the naive stage and how is this refined through teaching and experience? Peter Lee shows how children come to history with their own preconceptions. These involve 'ideas of time and change, of how we can know about the past, of how we explain historical events and processes, of what historical events are and why they so often differ'.[120] Without an understanding of how these concepts develop, teaching of history will be impoverished.

Tuning in

Basic motivational principles suggest that everything included in a curriculum should be included because it is worth learning for reasons that can be understood by the learners, and these reasons should be emphasized in introducing the content and scaffolding the activities that will be used to develop learning.

(Jere Brophy[121])

Experts make links, so part of expert teaching is to link what is being learned to what is already known. In terms of the comfort/learning/panic zone model it means we have to start in the comfort zone before we move into the learning zone in which new skills or understandings will be developed. This is an incremental process; move too quickly and it may be the panic zone for some students. John Hattie's analysis is that 'we need to already know about 90 per cent of what we are needing to master in order to make the most of the challenge', with reading having even higher levels of word knowledge.[122] We know that reading fluency is vital to comprehension. If readers are struggling to read the text, they will have little capacity for comprehending what they are reading. Effective 'tuning in' may also determine that our students know *more* than we think, often the case after transferring from primary to secondary school.

Tuning in: division in maths[123]

Students are asked to recall experiences of 'cutting things up' (cake, etc.) and relate them to division:

'So if you cut up the cake like this, how many pieces would you *divide it into?*'

Similarly the students' examples of 'sharing out' are linked to division:

'If there were six sweets to *divide* between two children, how many would each child get?'

So division is repeatedly linked to known concepts of sharing and cutting. So the question

'If a gardener has 20 bulbs to put equally in 5 flower beds, how many would be in each bed?'

is recognized as a sharing out problem and this means division.

Small stuff, but the learning here may be much deeper (or relational in SOLO terms) than it would be from a drill on how to divide. And in case that looks a bit elementary, try tuning yourself in as an adult to this problem:

> A woman is on a diet. She buys 3 turkey slices which weigh 1/3 of a pound but her diet only lets her eat 1/4 of a pound.
> How much of the 3 slices she bought can she eat if she stays on her diet?[124]

The interest here is less in the solution than how you went about it. How did you tune in (what kind of problem is this?) and did you find an elegant solution or was it a clunky one? This could have been presented as a worksheet simple fraction problem – but would that be as involving?

Learning intentions – let's be clear

One of the key expertise messages is that experts have a mental framework that allows them to see the big picture. John Wooden's coaching method does the same; you need to understand the whole move before you can learn the specific elements of it. In the classroom the teacher may have a picture of what is to be learned but this may not be the case for many students, like the bewildered 15-year-old in the opening quote. *Learning intentions* are a way of addressing this,[125] as they involve making explicit what is being learned. This is a lot harder than it looks. It's easy to say what we will be doing for the next 50 minutes but, in terms of Eraut's 'capacity change', what is it that we will learn from this activity? So we are painting rainbows this lesson – but what is the learning intention? Are we learning about the spectrum and refraction or colour mixing or developing hand–eye coordination or are we simply making something pretty for the fridge door?

Michael Absolum helps here by showing how we need to operate with layers of learning intentions, some of which are for the student and some for the teachers. His framework involves five levels, two for the teacher and three for the student (see box below). He summarizes these around a lesson on 'learning about paragraphs' – a topic so dull in isolation that passivity is just about guaranteed. But effectively linked to a bigger picture, more engagement is possible. So the teacher knows that the curriculum aim here is about improving communication skills (layer 1) and about shaping texts for a purpose (layer 2). For the student it is translated into 'writing a convincing argument' (layer 3), which involves developing an argument (layer 4) for which we will need paragraphs to organize it (layer 5).

Layers of learning intentions: introducing paragraphing[126]

1. *Big picture* – 'essence' – curriculum aim – 'by engaging with text-based activities become increasingly skilled speakers and writers'.

2. *Curriculum* – curriculum strand and level – 'show a developing understanding of how to shape (written) texts for different audiences and purposes . . .'.

3. *Translation of aim* – from prior assessment of students – 'we are learning to write an argument which is convincing'.

4. *Immediate learning* – 'we are learning to sequence an argument'.

5. *Specific learning* – 'we are learning what a paragraph is and when to start a new one'.

I'd want to begin this lesson by announcing that I was going to make the class, argumentative as they are, even better at arguing. To do that you need to build an argument, and that's where paragraphs come in. Richard Gerver has taken this even further by talking about TV soaps to show how they rapidly cut from one scene to another, and asking students about the intention behind this. This building towards a climax from different scenes is the tuning in for learning about paragraphs and how they each contribute to the message.[127] Good relational stuff, especially compared to students coming into the room to find on the board the learning intention of 'today we will learn about paragraphing'.

The key here is that the teacher knows where the lesson is going, and the students are being tuned in to the purpose of the lesson.

When learning intentions become unhelpful

Gary Klein, one of the foremost experts on decision-making, argues that an overreliance on procedures can erode expertise. This is because we get comfortable with procedures and may stop developing new skills or seeking to understand what we are doing. He gives the example of the extension of the Paris metro to Charles de Gaulle Airport. Because there were standard station designs and templates, the designers followed these – without thinking that this was an airport station and so travellers would have big suitcases. So no allowance was made and the results were chaotic, as people could not get their cases through the gates.

While recognizing the importance of procedures, Klein claims they don't always help us improve our performance since they encourage mediocre, rule-following behaviours. His position is, 'In complex situations, people will need judgment skills to follow procedures effectively and to go beyond them when necessary.'[128]

Procedures to give pupils a clear idea of what and why they are learning something are to be welcomed. However, in many schools writing up learning intentions for every lesson has become an institutional requirement, especially when senior leaders are checking for them, partly because the inspectorate will also be looking for them. This can easily turn them into a mindless routine. A true example here is a classroom in which the learning intentions were written on the board at the beginning of every lesson and the students were expected to write them down. With a school fair looming, a different teacher slipped in before the lesson and wrote in the usual learning objectives spot 'Don't forget to bring in your cakes tomorrow', which two-thirds of the class dutifully wrote down as the maths objective for the day. When routines are this dulling, even useful practices can become counterproductive.[129]

In their article 'The trouble with learning outcomes' Trevor Hussey and Patrick Smith argue that:

> while learning outcomes can be valuable if properly used, they have been misappropriated and adopted widely at all levels within the education system to facilitate the managerial process. This has led to their distortion . . . The proper interpretation of these outcomes must emerge from the context and prevailing activities and experiences of the students.[130]

Their focus is higher education, but their reminder is a salutary one: learning intentions are for the learners, not for senior leaders to check on what is being taught.

Keeping learning intentions meaningful requires expertise. This involves both the level at which they are pitched, as we saw with Michael Absolum's example, and when and how they are introduced. Learning intentions can be too vague to be helpful ('we are learning about the Middle Ages') or so specific that they encourage atomistic learning that does not see the bigger picture. This is a risk in preparing for tests and exams, when 'micro-teaching' that focuses on how to gain an extra mark here or there is presented in terms of highly specific learning objectives. Harry Torrance has made this point in relation to 'tick-a-box' approaches in many college vocational courses in which the challenge of deeper learning is replaced by 'criteria compliance' in which teachers and students seek ways to claim each of the dozens of criteria has been met.[131] The paradox here is that we can have met all the competencies without being competent. In terms of expertise this is because we have not developed the mental framework that integrates all these criteria and allows us to step back and assess what is needed. This was brought home to me by fire-service trainers who pointed out that firemen have to meet numerous health and safety competencies, yet for them the real test of competency was 'would you go up a ladder with that person?'

Refreshing learning intentions

Adaptive experts look for ways to keep learning intentions engaging for students. Do we always need to spell out what we are doing at the start of the lesson if we have a task that will puzzle and engage our students? After all, we wouldn't expect to have the solution to a detective novel given to us on the first page with the rest of the book simply explaining why. I asked one expert teacher how she managed to deal with management

> "Do we always need to spell out what we are doing at the start of the lesson if we have a task that will puzzle and engage our students?"

policy to put the learning intentions on the board at the start of each lesson. One of her strategies was writing the objectives and then covering them with a sheet of paper with a large question mark on it. She would then say to the class 'At the end of this lesson I want you to tell me what's under here.' Now there's adaptive expertise.

What does success look like?

John Wooden always demonstrated a move before he taught it. We would assume that in sport, you would not expect gymnasts to attempt a move without their knowing what it looked like ('Here's the manual; just follow the instructions'). Pick up any recent cookbook, no shortage of these, and there will be sumptuous photos of the dish – that's what your soufflé will, or should, look like. In music we would generally listen to a tune or song before we start practising it ourselves.

School subjects are no different, but when it comes to developing skills in general subjects such as English or history or maths, how well do we demonstrate what successful learning looks like? Royce Sadler, a central figure in feedback research,[132] has asked the question 'Why does thoughtful feedback often not work?' For him it's because learners often don't know what the required standard is, and if you don't know where you're trying to get to it's difficult to make use of feedback. It's like someone giving you directions when you don't know where you're going.

So how do we show students what a successful outcome would be? The first step might be to *negotiate* with them about what success might look like. Kathleen Gregory and colleagues provide a good example of a four-step model of how this might be done:[133]

Negotiating criteria for what is needed in a successful oral presentation

1. Brainstorm
2. Sort and categorize
3. Make and post a chart
4. Add, revise, refine

Here follows an example based on making a presentation.

Brainstorming (through class discussion with a list being written down):

- Look up and look at your audience/Have to be able to hear you/No fidgeting
- Look interested/Use small cards for notes/Make it interesting by using pictures or diagrams
- Use lots of expression/Slow down/Stand straight/Keep it short
- *Use specific examples to get your point across/Make sure you have a conclusion.*
- *We need to know what your topic is right away* [Teacher's contribution in italics]

Sort and categorize:

These are sorted, again through discussion, into a few major criteria and each suggestion put in a category:

S = speech and manner

I = interesting to audience

E = easy to follow

Make and post a chart. This will be the basis of any judgements about a presentation.

Interesting to an audience	Look interested Make it interesting by using pictures or diagrams

Easy to follow	Keep it short
	Use small cards for notes
	Slow down
	Use specific examples to get your point across
	Make sure you have a conclusion
	We need to know what your topic is right away
	Look up and look at your audience
	Have to be able to hear you
Speech and manner help the audience listen	No fidgeting
	Use lots of expression
	Stand straight

Add, revise, refine. At this stage the class takes a step back to see if this would work, whether more needs to be included or whether some editing is needed.

The intention in all this is to engage the students in understanding what an effective presentation would look like so that they will be to offer a more explicit assessment themselves. Reducing the list of criteria to three main elements makes any evaluation manageable and focuses on the central skills; it's no longer 'tick-a-box' compliance. This in turn will allow them to evaluate their own performance, developing the skill of self-assessment. In this example we see the teacher, who is more expert, contributing some of the key criteria that address the fundamentals: purpose, conclusion and examples. This is because the students, as novices, were drawn towards the surface features of a presentation.

Using examples

We may then need to provide *exemplars* of successful work. Sadler argues that an effective way of developing a sense of the required standard is to ask

> "If we can begin to recognize the quality of others' work, we can start to look at our own work in the same way."

students to compare two pieces of work, one at the standard, one that fell short. Using the agreed criteria, students are then asked to compare the work and judge which meets the standard and why. The purpose of this is to get a feel for the *quality* of the work. This is a vital part of learning self-assessment; if we can begin to recognize the quality of others' work, we can start to look at our own work in the same way.

There may be a concern here that providing examples like this may lead to students simply copying good examples. One way to lessen this problem may be to provide a series of different examples that meet the success criteria in varied ways, for example, different forms of writing in English.

This approach is at the heart of any apprenticeship model: working with those who are more skilled and seeing the quality of their work. If exemplars help to understand the standard involved, *modelling* becomes the way in which we show how to do it. What we learn from experts is that this is an essential part of improvement; writers initially model themselves on other writers, and performers on other performers. We saw that the Brontës' writing as children was highly derivative, as were Mozart's early compositions. Vincent van Gogh would trace classic Japanese prints in order to reproduce, and then modify, them. The same is true of Bob Dylan's musical progress. He was a highly effective 'borrower' and for years modelled himself on Woody Guthrie, even to the extent of dressing and talking like him. This was all part of his apprenticeship, from which he emerged to become his own creative force.

Modelling in practice: Sudoku

Do you know how to do Sudoku? If yes, using the example below, how would you explain how to do Sudoku to a colleague who doesn't? If no,

Fill in the grid so that each row, column and 3 x 3 box contains the numbers 1–9

			4	1	6			
		5					4	
	7							9
	6			3				5
		8			6			
2			1				9	
1								2
	3	4					7	
			3	7	9			

Figure 3 Sudoku: modelling the process

how would you make sense of this puzzle and work out how to do it? The point here is that just reading out the instructions is rarely sufficient. Simple though they are, it is hard to make sense of them without someone modelling what a completed puzzle would involve and demonstrating the processes involved. This is likely to be more than a verbal exercise: we invariably need to show what we mean. It's also no use just giving the solution ('put 4 here'), as without understanding this can't help us learn.

The parallel with the classroom comes with the assumption that giving clear instructions, and Sudoku instructions are very clear, is enough for learners to understand what they need to do. Understanding requires more than this; we have to model and exemplify what the process is – how do we go about successfully completing a puzzle?

Deliberate practice

At the heart of expertise is extensive purposeful practice that converts what is originally difficult into something that is fluent and, at best, automatic. So sporting experts make difficult moves look easy and soloists play whole symphonies 'in the flow' without the music in front of them. This looks effortless because the effort has gone into many hours of focused practice: Ericsson's *iceberg illusion*.

> ❝At the heart of expertise is extensive purposeful practice that converts what is originally difficult into something that is fluent and, at best, automatic.❞

We don't have that many hours in the classroom, but I think we are sometimes in such a hurry to cover the curriculum that we fail to embed new skills sufficiently. Howard Gardner makes the point:

> The greatest enemy of understanding is coverage. As long as you are determined to cover everything, you actually ensure that most kids are not going to understand. You've got to take enough time to get kids deeply involved in something so they can think about it in lots of different ways and apply it – not just at school but at home and on the street and so on.[134]

How many of us pick up a new computing skill with only a single run-through or are able to use all the options on our mobile phone after a single look at the manual? We have to practise quite deliberately to get the hang of these, and I bet we've all missed an opportunity, a call or a photo, because we couldn't work out quickly enough what to do.

Gardner's 'thinking about it in lots of different ways' is part of *mindful* practice. To practise a new learning by giving 20 very similar maths problems to solve encourages mindless work – just do the same thing each time. Five problems that come at the same skill from a variety of angles, each one needing some thought, are far more effective in encouraging understanding.

So here's a good historical example of combining modelling and deliberate practice. Benjamin Franklin is recognized as one of America's first great men of letters. He was remarkable by any standards. Having left school at 10 to become an apprentice printer, he developed into a true polymath, contributing to science (electricity, [remember the kite?] meteorology, identifying the Gulf Stream), to politics as a founding father of the United States, Ambassador to France and Governor of Pennsylvania, a chess champion and a composer. And much more.[135] He had enjoyed writing letters as a teenager and had used the pseudonym of Mrs Dogood to write letters to the local newspaper on which he worked as printer. These were popular, but he wasn't, when found out, resulting in a hasty move to Philadelphia at age 17. He was also involved in a teenage correspondence with a friend over whether women should be educated – Benjamin thought they should. His father looked at these exchanges and gave the feedback that Benjamin was better at spelling and punctuation than at organizing and presenting his argument. See his response in the box below.

Benjamin Franklin (1706–90): deliberate practice in action[136]

The young Franklin searched out a model of good argumentative writing and selected a volume of the *Spectator* magazine. As he read an article, he made brief notes of every sentence and would then, some days later, try to write the sentences in his own words. He then 'discovered some of my faults and corrected them'.

He noticed that one of his weaknesses was poor vocabulary and knew that poetry required an extensive 'stock of words', so he would rewrite the articles in verse. He would later take the verse and rewrite it as prose, again comparing them to the original.

He also realized that organization is important in essay writing, so he would make notes on each *Spectator* sentence on separate pieces of paper, mix them up, come back to them after several weeks and put them in order, when he 'discovered many faults and amended them'.

In case we're tempted to put this down to the work of a bored teenager with time on his hands, a reminder that Franklin was in full-time employment, so he practised before he went to work, at night and on Sunday, often missing church because he could not 'afford time' to go.

Seeing the big picture

Experts have a mental framework that helps them size up a situation and develop strategies to deal with it. Expert teachers also have to be able to communicate this to their students, so they too know what they are learning and why. The aim here is to help learners make meaning out of what they are being asked to learn. Expert teachers have developed the adaptive expertise that allows them to 'tune in' to their students and make clear to them what is being learned – John Hattie's 'visible learning'. Central to this are clear learning intentions, which must avoid the dulling routine of explicit objectives on every board in every lesson. Accompanying this is how we show our students what successful work

"Expert teachers have developed the adaptive expertise that allows them to 'tune in' to their students and make clear to them what is being learned."

will look like through exemplars, modelling and practice. In this way we encourage students to become expert learners themselves.

For us to be able to 'tune in' effectively and help learners move towards the standard we want, we must first know where they are in their learning so that we can build on this. This is the theme of the next chapter.

Questions for discussion

1. Discuss the policies on learning intentions in your context. What are some strategies for keeping learning intentions engaging and effective?

2. A good way to experience what the SOLO is like in practice is three high quality eight-minute videos on YouTube *Teaching Teaching and Understanding Understanding* on http://www.youtube.com/watch?v=ggThtlnFtnM (accessed 2 Aug. 2013), which introduce Biggs's work at university level. How could these practices be transferred to your own situation?

3. This group activity encapsulates many of the practices that have been looked at in this chapter – it's an activity that repays a few minutes of play – even for those who 'don't do puzzles'.

   Use the example from p.98 to find out who knows how to do Sudoku and who doesn't. The learning intention is for everyone to understand how to approach any Sudoku puzzle. The task is to team up so that those who know (greens) can work with those who don't (reds). Do this for 5 to 10 minutes and then consider the following:

   • Why had greens learned Sudoku and how would they persuade reds it was worthwhile? (Tuning in.)

- Why didn't reds know how to do it? What had stopped them learning earlier?

- The instructions are short and in simple English yet difficult for the novice – why?

- How was this *modelled* for the learner?

- What strategies did reds learn? How was self-regulation encouraged?

- How could this transfer to classroom learning?

5

Expert Diagnosis: The Teacher as Clinician

The most important single factor influencing learning is what the learner already knows. Ascertain this and teach him accordingly.

(David Ausubel[137])

One of the foundations of modern learning theory is that we learn more effectively when we build on what we know. We saw this in earlier chapters in moving from the comfort zone to the learning zone and in linking new information to what we already know in deep learning approaches. As adults we could learn serviceable French in a month, but to learn serviceable Mandarin Chinese would take years. Why? Because there's nothing to build on; the characters, notation, tonal structure and grammar are all different (so hats off to all those Chinese-speaking students who have learned English). So, to pitch our teaching where students can learn, rather than staying in the comfort zone or being pushed into the panic zone, we need to find out what they know and can do. To do this we need good diagnostic skills.

Expert diagnosis

Teachers are not alone in having to diagnose where somebody is. This is a central part of expertise in medicine, sport and other occupations where decision-making is essential. In this chapter we look at the parallels between expert classroom teaching and other expert diagnosis, particularly medical, and see what we might learn from these. Medical diagnosis has been described as 'an inferential process, carried out under conditions of uncertainty, often with incomplete and sometimes inconsistent information'.[138]

This could just as well be a definition of classroom diagnostics. Here too we work with limited information – we too may have test information, observation and dialogue that will allow us a best guess at how a student understands something, yet we know that our information may well not do justice to the learner.

When it comes to diagnosis and decision-making, teachers have much in common with other experts who deal with dynamic situations in which complex information has to be analysed and acted upon immediately. Teaching may not be as dramatic as a medical emergency or air traffic control, but the principles are the same. All exhibit *cognitive complexity*, which demands deliberate cognitive processing in addition to routine or automatic processing. Given we can only manage a limited amount of complexity, how we manage this is a function of expertise.

The box below summarizes some of the main findings on decision-making in pressure situations.

Expert diagnostic decision-making[139]

Experts in urgent decision-making situations do the following:

1. Act rapidly, using previous experience, immediate feedback and careful monitoring and assessment of the situation. This links back to the expert's extensive knowledge base and its organization.

2. Use a process of *serial-evaluation* of options, in which they rapidly choose what seems to be the best one and work forward until the feedback and monitoring don't support it, at which point they consider another option. This is an approach that has been found across chess grandmasters, clinicians, the military and emergency services.

   (Less experienced decision-makers tend systematically to introduce a range of options at the start and deliberately weigh up which course of action seems the best.)

3. Focus on the *symptoms*, select what looks the best option and use mental simulations to evaluate it. 'This is a function of a highly structured knowledge base and well-developed pattern recognition capabilities' (p.133). For example, experienced triage nurses learn to recognize critical symptoms that evoke rule-of-thumb diagnostic decisions.

   (Novices tend to employ 'backward reasoning' in which they develop several hypotheses and then test them against the data, often failing to evaluate each of them systematically.)

4. Use pattern recognition, which allows the expert to spot anomalies in the information that others overlook and that are major diagnostic clues. This is at the heart of medical series such as *House M.D.*, in which the grumpy and generally unpleasant Gregory House (Hugh Laurie) regularly spots discrepancies that his eager young and knowledgeable team miss.

Applications for the classroom

Part of a teacher's skill is to determine where learners are in their learning as the foundation for new learning. Studies of medical expertise show us just how important dialogue and effective questioning are in this – something that is often neglected in education. This section looks at some of the key features of diagnosis: making oral work central, developing effective questioning and dealing with wrong answers.

Underestimating the oral

Lisa Sanders points out that in medicine 'talking to the patient more often than not provides the essential clues to making a diagnosis. Moreover, what we learn from this simple interview frequently plays an important role in the patient's health even after the diagnosis is made.'[140] As a diagnostic tool, what the patient says is often more important than high-tech tests and even the physical exam in providing crucial information. So why, in the classroom, do we place so little emphasis on higher-order discussions?

> "As a diagnostic tool, what the patient says is often more important than high-tech tests and even the physical exam in providing crucial information."

Robin Alexander has compared classroom cultures across the world and observes, 'In England more than in many other countries, an educational culture has evolved in which writing is viewed as the only "real" school work'.[141] So, for many of us, the idea of going a whole lesson just discussing a topic means we never really got down to work. Yet language and thought are intimately related, with cognitive development depending on language. He found that in classrooms in many other countries in Europe:

- there is more emphasis on oracy;
- the purpose of classroom talk is seen as mainly cognitive – in England it is primarily social and affective ('communication skills');
- questions are designed to encourage reasoning and speculation – with longer exchanges;
- making mistakes is intrinsic to learning rather than a matter for shame.

In Jacky Lumby's research one of the most frequent complaints of disengaged and disaffected teenagers was about 'long stretches of time . . . listening to the teacher or reading instructions and then writing', with a typical comment being 'I hate it. It's writing every single day. It's all day. It's every single lesson.'[142] These were the students who felt they learned best through experiential learning such as 'discussion in, for example, religious education and philosophy and ethics', interestingly the very areas that encourage higher-order discussion.

How good are our questions?

Part of the skill of diagnosis is to ask the right questions. If we want to establish what someone knows, we need to ask questions that will inform our current best guess. Simply asking a question and seeing if pupils get the correct answer may not tell us what we need to know – they may get the right answer for the wrong reason and the wrong answer for the right reason. So here's an example from an international maths study:[143]

Which fraction is smallest: $\frac{1}{6}$; $\frac{2}{3}$; $\frac{1}{3}$; $\frac{1}{2}$?

Some 88 per cent of 11-year-olds got this right, so we might conclude that they have understood basic fractions. However, the additional question

Which fraction is largest: $\frac{4}{5}$; $\frac{3}{4}$; $\frac{5}{8}$; $\frac{7}{10}$?

produced only 46 per cent of correct answers, with 39 per cent choosing the same wrong answer.

So what's the diagnosis? Have a lot of these 11-year-olds worked with a rule that the bigger the bottom number, the smaller the fraction and then used the inverse rule so that the smaller the bottom number the bigger the fraction? This might explain why 39 per cent chose the same wrong answer ($\frac{3}{4}$). So we diagnose that many pupils are ignoring the top part of the fraction, the numerator, and have a fair way to go in understanding fractions.

Most of us probably feel that we do ask the kinds of probing questions that would get at such misunderstandings. However, the evidence doesn't offer much support. For example, John Hattie has researched and analysed teacher–pupil interactions and come up with these uncomfortable findings:[144]

- teachers talk 70–80 per cent of the time;
- teachers ask 200–300 questions a day of which 60 per cent require recall of facts and 20 per cent are procedural ('where's your book?');

- less than 5 per cent of the time is spent in group or whole class discussion of meaningful ideas;
- 70 per cent of answers take students less than five seconds and, on average, involve three words.

These findings have been replicated in other studies, and have not changed much in over a century.[145] The major Junior School Project in England had even more chilling statistics. It found that over two-thirds of the teachers observed made no use of open-ended questions. Over a three-year period only 1 per cent of observed lessons was devoted to questions requiring problem solving, though there were considerable differences between teachers.[146]

We can also stir into the pot Mary Rowe's findings that on average teachers wait for less than a second after having asked a question before they do something – identify a respondent, rephrase it or answer it.[147]

The research on questioning points to some clear findings:

1. At all ages a combination of lower-order questions (remembering) and higher-order (thinking) seems most effective.

2. The percentage of higher-order questions should increase with age (50 per cent plus at age 10 onwards).

The idea of half our questions being higher-order links to the higher cognitive demands made by expert teachers (p.68–9), though this may be a long way from current practice. Most research suggests less than a tenth of classroom questions are higher order. Ted Wragg, who found only 8 per cent of these kinds of questions, commented, 'Because teachers ask so many questions in a day, it's easy for one style of questioning to become habitual . . . and lower order questions feel safest because they keep the lesson moving.'[148]

Rich questioning

So what kinds of questions can we use to move classroom discussion to a higher-order level and to provide better diagnostics of what learners understand? Going back to the SOLO taxonomy, higher-order questions will be aiming at synthesizing information ('relational') and encouraging generalizations and links to other concepts ('extended abstract'). So we would expect to see question stems such as *'why does . . .?'; 'what if . . .?'; 'how would you . . .?'; 'could you explain . . .?'* Here are some of my favourites. Your task is to think what lower-order question they replaced and what kind of thinking they are encouraging.

Examples of rich questions

1. How would a tourist and a homeless person see York/London/wherever differently?
2. If you keep a drink with ice in a thermos (vacuum) flask, do you need to leave the room for the ice cubes to melt?
3. Describe what a poem is.
4. Would putting a coat on a snowman help to stop it melting?
5. How reliable is a school report?

A brief comment on the last two: I like the snowman question because it can't be answered until the teacher has been in a dialogue (what kind of coat? Where is it? What's the temperature?), or, if it is answered yes or no, the teacher can come back with plenty of 'what if' questions to challenge a simplistic answer. The last question was a good example of tuning in for a history project; the school report question led into a consideration of how reliable documentary evidence is.[149]

It's not just what we ask but how we ask

We can ask very good questions in a way that doesn't encourage much thinking in the classroom. The most familiar of these ways is to focus questioning on those who are keen to answer (and who will often be sitting in the front few rows). So the rest of the class know there will be volunteers and can remain passive. This is encouraged even more when I get locked into an enthusiastic dialogue with a particular student: 'Oh yes, marvellous answer. How did you arrive at that?'

Some strategies that limit this blinkered exchange with just one or two students involve limiting the emotionality of our response and making sure we move any discussion around the room. The first of these practices is the *poker-face*: I get an exciting answer but stay neutral and open it up: 'Thank you. Any comments on this, or any disagreement?' This leads to the second practice of passing answers around the group for further elaboration. The mantra here is 'basketball not ping-pong' – this is not two players going backwards and forwards, but a room in which the ball has to be skilfully moved round as many people as possible while at the same time deepening the discussion.

Wait time

We learned from Mary Rowe's research the importance of allowing some thinking time.[150] What kind of question takes less than a second to process and respond to? Probably a recall or 'what have I just said?' one. She also found that even waiting three seconds for low-level recall questions and ten seconds for higher-order questions significantly improved responses, while pausing *after* an answer was given allowed students to revise their answers or for others to contribute. Are we, as teachers, too anxious about silence to allow it to be productive? Here's a comment from a teacher who changed his practice:

> Increasing waiting time after asking questions proved difficult to start with – due to my habitual desire to 'add' something almost immediately after asking the original question. The pause after asking the question was sometimes 'painful'. It felt unnatural to have such a seemingly 'dead' period but I persevered. . . . Now, after many months of changing my style of questioning I have noticed that most students will give an answer and an explanation (where necessary) without additional prompting.[151]

 American research on encouraging higher-order thinking skills in disadvantaged students has provided similar findings. It can be productive but it takes time: 'It takes about four months before students will give a reason for a response without being asked, and it takes about six months before they will disconfirm a prior answer.'[152]

Time-outs

The most powerful practice at this point is that of pairing up students to discuss a response briefly ('pair and share'). The logic here is that if everybody has discussed a response, I can ask anybody in the room. So I don't need volunteers to put up their hands; I can ask anybody, so the whole class has to stay active. Indeed, I may use a random process to select a respondent – some teachers use a jar containing lolly sticks with names on and draw blind. Answering becomes the luck of the draw, so I'd better be ready. I've also seen this work really well with teacher group discussions, where one group would be randomly selected to give a presentation at the end. That focused the mind and reduced the usual group chat.

Wrong answers

While on most days the classroom may lack the drama of an emergency ward, the diagnostic decision-making principles still hold. Most of our interactions are immediate: we have to respond quickly to our students. When we've asked a question and got an unlikely answer from a pupil, what do we do next? The temptation is to thank the pupil and move on to 'anybody else got an answer?' until we get the one we want. We sometimes justify this in terms of protecting the self-esteem of the pupil who got it wrong, an approach that goes against the risk taking and failure that are part of developing expertise. A more constructive perspective is that provided by Reuven Feuerstein and colleagues:

> Error cannot be viewed solely as failure: rather, its source must be sought. In doing so the teacher demonstrates their respect for the student as a thinking being who has arrived at a response through reasons that may not correspond to the task, but which, nonetheless, exist and must be explored.[153]

I find this helpful; it encourages us, out of respect, to tease out the student's thinking. Good diagnostics might also involve 'Who else thinks this?' to see how widely a misunderstanding may be shared.

So passing over the 'wrong' answer is unhelpful to the first pupil who, no doubt, had given what seemed to her a correct answer. As diagnosticians we can see this as a symptom of some different thinking or misunderstandings that we need to know about if we are to help learning. Going back to the earlier example of naive scientific thinking (p.64) we might have asked the class about why we have winter and summer. The answer that the sun is further away in the winter might alert us to beliefs that the sun moves round the earth. This would be our pattern recognition. Our serial-processing would be to follow up on this with some further questions – 'Why is it summer in Australia at the same time?' or 'Why is it darker in the winter?' These are our 'triage' questions to diagnose what the understanding is here.

Herbert Ginsburg provides an example of good diagnostics, the teacher following up on a wrong answer:

'How much is 7 – 4?' Becky (age 6): '2'
    'How did you get that answer?'
    'I knew that 7 take away 4 is 2 because I knew 4 + 2, is 7. And if 4 plus 2 is 7, then 7 take away 2 must be 4.'
    The second ingredient in the cognitive stew was more interesting than the faulty memory. She introduced the idea that if 4 + 2 = 7 *then it must be true that* 7 – 4 = 2 . . . A classic syllogism.[154]

> "Sometimes one further 'why' or 'how' question may unlock how a pupil is thinking."

How easy would it have been to say 'Thank you Becky. Does anybody have a different answer?' Instead, a good diagnostic question means we learn Becky is mathematically sophisticated for her age, while needing to improve basic computation. Sometimes one further 'why' or 'how' question may unlock how a pupil is thinking.

Here's another rich example, this time about language. Two 7-year-olds have been studying the reproductive cycle of frogs. The teacher asks them to write up what they have learned from the classroom conversation. James writes, 'When frogs are born there called frogs born and there in little rond bits of jelly so they con't do nofing.' Emily writes, 'Tadpole and frog.

I already new that frog's have Baby's. I have learnt that tadpole come out of frog's sporn.' Gunter Kress points out that these comments reveal a lot about the children. First of all, they are 'meticulous phoneticians recording the sounds of north London' who, when faced with an unfamiliar word, took different routes. James took the route of *meaning*: 'frogs born' is how frogs come into life. Emily's route is via grammar, such as 'mum's bag', a sporn must be something frogs have. Kress comments:

> Here lies my unease. Of course I think James and Emily should learn to spell frogspawn the 'correct' way. But on their road to that goal I worry that we overlook and lose their energy, precision and eagerness to encounter the unknown and make sense of it. I worry that our present educational paths may be stifling, not fostering, their exuberance and creativity.[155]

Are we listening?

The majority of medical diagnoses are made on the basis of the patient's story alone. When we go to the doctor, we are usually asked what brought us there, and we usually have a story to tell, one we will already have rehearsed with family and friends. This is vital to diagnosis, but, claims Lisa Sanders, 'the odds are overwhelming that the patient won't have much of an opportunity to tell that story'.[156] Why? Because a 'facts only' attitude will mean doctors are likely to interrupt with interrogation questions. Even when being taped, research revealed that doctors interrupted their patients 75 per cent of the time. In one study, doctors listened for an average of 16 seconds before breaking in, some interrupting the patient after only three seconds. 'Once the story was interrupted, patients were unlikely to resume it. In these recorded encounters fewer than 2 per cent of the patients completed their story once the doctor broke in.'

I don't know of any similar research in teaching, but my guess is that there will be parallels. When I worked as an educational psychologist, in a privileged position of often being one-to-one with a student for a chunk of time, I realized that teachers rarely heard a pupil out. More often they would interrupt with an interpretation of how they saw it. Like being anxious about silence, teachers have a habit of quickly jumping in with 'you should' and 'you must' well before they know the full story. Better to wait and probe – but much harder. When I was teaching, I'm sure I learned more about children's thinking from eavesdropping while driving my children and their friends than I did from the students in my class, whom I didn't have time to listen to.

Summary

Diagnostics for teaching – the importance of dialogue

- Talk is our best diagnostic tool – as it is in medicine.
- We underestimate the value of talk in an educational culture in which 'real work' is based on writing.

- Good diagnosis relies on rich questions that elicit learners' higher-order thinking.
- Learners need thinking time, with discussion in pairs a powerful way of involving the whole class.
- We need to listen and to hear our students out.
- Wrong answers are an important source of diagnostic information when respectfully followed up.

Expert learners as questioners

Once you have learned to ask questions – relevant and appropriate and substantial – you have learned how to learn and no one can keep you from learning whatever it is you need to know.

(Postman and Weingartner[157])

So far this chapter has focused on teachers as expert questioners, yet an essential part of learning expertise is to be able to ask questions that help make sense of what we are trying to understand. Young children do this all the time, but by the time they reach secondary school they've virtually stopped. What has happened along the way that makes students unlikely to ask higher-order questions? As the story goes, Einstein's mother always asked him, 'What questions did you ask today?', rather than the usual 'What did you do in school today?' – and we know where that got him.

So how can students be encouraged to ask higher-order questions? The first step is that teachers are asking them as well, modelling question-asking, including not always knowing the answer. We also need classrooms in which students are not afraid to ask a question because they may look ignorant or foolish. Mike Hughes gives an example from a class he observed that was looking at the causes of the 1985 Mexico City earthquake.[158] The text read *'the earthquake was caused by movement along the subduction zone . . .'* and the key question was 'What caused the earthquake in Mexico City?' The correct answer, which all the class got, was 'movement along the subduction zone'. But nobody knew what a subduction zone was – *and nobody asked*. So we've learned about earthquakes and understood very little. 'What would Einstein have asked?' might be a useful wall poster and refrain here.

If students are inhibited about asking questions in the full class, we may want to begin with group work. This may start with asking small groups a question to work on but then move to the groups generating their own questions, which they may then ask other groups.[159] The teachers involved in Assessment for Learning action research, with a team from King's College, developed this approach with students, who set questions and marked answers, with some questions even being used in class tests. One of the teachers commented:

> Pupils setting their own questions has proved to be a stimulating and productive means of rounding off topics and revising their work. Answering other people's questions and discussing solutions with the whole class is a very effective way of concentrating on topics that need to be revised rather than spending time on what is already known. Students have had to think about what makes a good question for a test and in doing so need to have a clear understanding of the subject material.[160]

A more general extension of this is that students work in groups to ask questions about a topic, particularly about any parts they don't understand. This is a subtle, and powerful, difference from a teacher's questions, which may often be driven by the need to check those things that are known.

Encouraging individual questioning

To overcome individual reticence to ask questions we may need to look for less direct ways of doing this. One is to ask students to write down a question in response to a report or presentation. This is put in a question box, from which questions will be drawn randomly. A similar device is an 'Ask teacher' box into which students can deposit questions as they leave at the end of the lesson and which the teacher responds to in the next lesson.

This can be kick-started by requiring every student to hand in a question when leaving the room.

Mike Hughes has developed some role plays that encourage individual questioning. Students may be given the role of newspaper reporters and each has to prepare a question to ask a visiting expert, who could be the teacher, a student who has researched the topic or a genuine visiting expert. So in relation to the Mexico City earthquake, the instructions would be along the lines of 'you know very little about earthquakes so you will have to do some research before you fly to Mexico. The editor has arranged for an expert to visit the office . . . please make sure you have prepared some questions in advance.' This may seemed contrived – but how many of us would find it easier to stand up and sing in public in a role (impersonating, in disguise, etc.) than as ourselves?

Becoming the expert

Learners assume that teachers know the answers to any questions they ask, otherwise why would they ask them? Some expert modelling would be to ask some questions we don't know the answer to and get our students to investigate. A good Google will generate plenty of answers – and a good discussion as these are sifted through. This is what many expert clinicians do when faced with illness they can't diagnose. Lisa Sanders provides a case study of a patient with persistent nausea who had already run the gamut of specialist diagnosis and every test in the book, all to no avail. The young doctor who was seeing her this time listened to her story and registered that the patient said that she felt well only when she was in a hot shower. This strange detail was not dismissed; instead, she Googled 'persistent nausea improved by hot showers'. Within a few seconds she was learning about a disease she had never heard of that was associated with chronic marijuana use, which further questioning established was the case for this patient.[161]

121

Stating the obvious – but not doing it

We recognize the importance of good classroom dialogue, of rich questioning and investigating misunderstandings, and of encouraging our students to ask questions. But the research shows that in practice we rarely achieve this. One occupational hazard is that we are not good with pauses and silence (unless our students are doing the 'real work' of copying and writing). It may also be that we want to spare our students the embarrassment of wrong answers rather than seeing them as respectful ways into understanding the students' thinking. And, of course, we have to keep things moving at a pace and not get distracted into deep discussions that could take up too much lesson time. If we want our students to be questioning, we have to model this. What would Einstein have asked?

Questions for discussion

1. How can you audit the questions/answers/dialogue in your classroom or school? How do you predict the findings would stack up against the research claims?

2. How can you monitor wait time in our classrooms? What happens if you progressively extend it? (Do our questions change?)

3. Are your students willing to ask higher-order questions? What seems to encourage this in your classes?

4. Do you see merit in implementing practices such as role play, 'unknown' research questions, exit questions, question boxes? If you were to introduce one, which would it be? Why?

6

Getting and Giving Feedback: It's Harder Than We Think

> We believe that researchers and practitioners alike confuse their feelings that feedback is desirable with the question of whether Feedback . . . benefits performance.
>
> (Avraham Kluger and Angelo DeNisi[162])

> If I had to reduce all of the research on feedback into one simple overarching idea, at least for academic subjects in school, it would be this: feedback should cause thinking.
>
> (Dylan Wiliam[163])

One of the hallmarks of expert learning is receiving effective feedback. John Wooden's feedback methods as a basketball coach were so effective that they were studied in depth by educational researchers who then developed successful teaching schemes based on them.[164] One of the distinctive features of his approach was that most feedback came as players practised; he didn't go in for long harangues or 'chalk talks' but rather 'short, punctuated, and numerous' comments to players as they played. The researchers coded these over many practices and found that three-quarters of the 2000-plus utterances were *pure information*: what to do, how to do it, when to intensify the activity. Less than 7 per cent were compliments, the same proportion as for expressions of displeasure. His most frequent form of feedback was to model the right way to do something, show the incorrect way, and then model the correct way again, all in a matter of a few seconds.

We all give and get a lot of feedback, but most of it doesn't close the gap between current and desired performance and it is as likely to widen the learning gap as to close it. This chapter's opening comment from Kluger and DeNisi was a conclusion from their meta-analysis of the research on feedback, which also found that 'In over one third of the cases Feedback Interventions reduced performance.' This chapter looks at what we've learned about effective feedback – and what we know doesn't work.

Feedback often works in unintended ways. We can give the same feedback to two students and it will help one and set learning back for the other. So we can say 'this is wrong' to experts and this may be enough – they will draw on their process skills and self-regulation to investigate. Say the same to novices and they may decide they are no good at this and give up.

What would you expect the reaction to be to a school report that offers the following feedback to a 15-year-old?

This has been a disastrous half [year]. His work has been far from satisfactory. His prepared stuff has been badly learned . . . and several times he has been in trouble because he will not listen, but will insist on doing his work in his own way. I believe [he] has ideas about becoming a scientist; on his present form this is quite ridiculous; if he can't learn simple biological facts, he would have no chance doing the work of a specialist and it would be a sheer waste of time, both on his part and those who teach him.[165]

This was a student who had scored the lowest mark for biology in his year and he commented 'out of 250 people, to come bottom of the bottom form is quite something, and in a way the most remarkable achievement I could have been said to make'. This student was Sir John Gurdon, the 2012 Nobel Prize winner in . . . yes, you've guessed, biology. He keeps a framed copy of this report on his wall and comments, 'When you have problems, like an experiment doesn't work, which often happens, it's nice to remind yourself that perhaps after all you're not so good at this job, and the schoolmaster might have been right.'[166]

And what would you predict for the 400 11-year-olds given a series of simple puzzles, for which they were given their score plus six words of feedback? Half were praised for intelligence ('you must be smart at this'), and the other half were praised for effort ('you must have worked really hard'). They were then given a choice of whether to take an easy or hard test, after which they then all took a test so hard that none succeeded, followed by a chance to do a further test similar to the first one.

The results showed that the wording of the feedback made a big difference. Two-thirds of those praised for their intelligence chose the easier test option while 90 per cent of those praised for effort chose the hard one. On the 'impossible' task the group praised for effort persevered longer, enjoyed it more, and did not appear to suffer any loss in confidence, while the group praised for intelligence interpreted failure as proof they were no good at puzzles after all. On the final test, a similar one to the first, the intelligence group showed a 20 per cent decline in score, while the effort group showed a 30 per cent increase. This was all the result of four different words in their feedback.[167] In a series of follow-up investigations, students were told that the same study was going to be done in another school and were asked to record their thoughts about the tasks. They were also asked to put how many problems they got right on each set of problems. All but one of the effort feedback group told the truth, whereas a full 40 per cent of the praised-for-intelligence group lied about their scores. This looks like a case of protecting reputations, an extension of the laddish tendency to do the required work badly or not at all, and then to claim they had the ability but just hadn't bothered. We shall return to what makes feedback to students effective or ineffective.

Teachers getting feedback

As teachers we are bombarded with feedback from our students about what they can or can't do, what they have engaged with, and what is of little interest. In the previous chapter we looked at how good diagnostic work, particularly through classroom dialogue, provided all sorts of feedback about student understandings and misconceptions. For this feedback to work we have to do something about it. We can always ignore it, usually by blaming the students for not understanding – 'I've taught them but they just won't learn.' However, as we saw earlier, experts are continually monitoring their performance and are self-critical, looking for what may not have worked. Atul Gawande provides an example of this in the gloomily named 'Morbidity and Mortality (M&M) Conferences' that take place on a weekly basis in most American teaching hospitals. In these, medics gather behind closed doors to 'review the mistakes, untoward events, and deaths that occurred on their watch, determine responsibility, and figure out what to do differently next time'.[168] The incidents are selected by the more junior residents but presented, in a 'bloodless and compact' way, by the senior responsible medic. M&M is not a trial, so names are not named. The intention is to learn from what went wrong. Do we have any parallel process in schools?

Expert reflection is also an individual process. In their major *Learning How to Learn* project Mary James and colleagues found that the teachers who understood the underlying principles of assessment for learning were far more critical of their own teaching than those teachers with a limited grasp of them, who were quicker to blame the students.[169] This is an interesting paradox: those committed to creating self-regulated learners were harder on themselves when it didn't happen.

The key question for teachers is 'What do we do when we get feedback?' Feedback is effective only if we act on it, so should lead to changes in how we teach. For example, we get feedback from any classroom assignment or test. If we use the information diagnostically, we may see that some of our teaching was unsuccessful, and we may need to go back and modify our teaching. Expert teachers also spot patterns: here is a topic that regularly proves difficult for students. David Carless has called this *pre-emptive formative assessment* in which we recognize that previous students have had difficulty with a topic, so we need to adjust our teaching for our current ones. So if the exam marks last year, or for several years, have been lower on a particular topic, we need to adjust our teaching rather than just lament 'children nowadays . . .'.[170]

Once again I'm stating the obvious, but how many of us teachers respond to such feedback by substantially revising our approach to a tricky topic we teach regularly? One model for this kind of revision is that of the *study lesson* in Japan, where teachers regularly come together to develop *one* lesson, often the introduction to a difficult topic, for example, fractions. They may spend a year researching, developing and piloting this lesson that then becomes public, with other teachers invited to watch it.[171] Modified forms of this are being introduced in collaborative work across schools in the UK.[172]

Teachers giving feedback

To be effective, feedback needs to be clear, purposeful, meaningful, and compatible with students' prior knowledge and to provide logical connections.

(Hattie and Timperley[173])

"How effective is our feedback? There's been a good deal of research on this, all of which suggests there is no simple formula for getting it right."

We're probably happier giving rather than receiving feedback. How effective is our feedback? There's been a good deal of research on this, all of which suggests there is no simple formula for getting it right.[174] Can you think of an example of feedback that worked for you in moving your learning forward? What was it that made this feedback effective?

My guess is that it was an interaction of elements including timing, respect for the person giving it, the quality of the feedback and a wish to improve. My own answer would come from sports coaching – those expert instructors who can spot what's going wrong and can focus on a specific activity that will correct a problem. So as a 'rustic' downhill skier, lacking the graceful flow of those gliding past me, my diagonal turns (because I don't dare go directly down steep hills) are the sort a tractor would make. One problem is that this is exhausting: grinding to a halt and then changing direction. Enter an expert instructor who simply says: 'Let's do Ss rather than Zs – follow me'; so rather than banging on the brakes at each turn I learn to use the turn and the hill to control my speed and to keep me in the learning, rather than panic, zone. I've had other coaches that point out the dozen-plus things I'm doing wrong – 'you need to lean your shoulder, bend your knees, put your weight . . .' – that leave me skiing, and feeling, much worse. It's too much to take in when you're a nervous novice.

We do know that there are features that make it more likely to be successful. These are summarized below and then developed in more detail.

Features of effective feedback

1. It is clearly linked to the learning intention.

2. The learner understands the success criteria/standard.

3. It focuses on the task rather than the learner (self/ego).

4. It gives cues at appropriate levels on how to bridge the gap.

5. It is effectively timed.

6. It is specific and clear.

7. It offers strategies rather than solutions.

8. It challenges, requires action and is achievable.

Feedback is clearly linked to the learning intention

This seems obvious: if we are helping students to learn something our feedback will focus on this. So, for example, the learning intention is *to create 'mood-setting' in writing through our descriptions.* The (negotiated) success criterion is 'We will be able to recognize the mood the writer was creating' and the task is 'Write an opening paragraph that describes a place in a way that sets the mood for a story.' What one line of feedback would you give this student?

> The wind howled thrugh the stretes and the rain bownced of the pavements. The few people who were out huried head down from doorway to doorway. All escept one man who, coatless and uprite carried a big wet bag.

I use this as my 'red rag to a bull' example. The intention was creative mood setting, something at which the student has been reasonably successful. Yet how many of us would have given feedback on spelling, punctuation and grammar rather than improving the evocative quality of the paragraph? Yes, they need improving – but this was not the learning intention, we can do a further draft that attends to these. Shirley Clarke makes the point that we regularly mislead children; we say we're looking for one thing and then assess for something different.[175] Staying with the learning intention is not as simple as it seems.

The learner understands the success criteria/standard

This feature was addressed in Chapter 4: if we don't know what we're trying to achieve, we won't be able to make much sense of any feedback. Mihali Csikszentmihalyi has introduced the idea of *flow* – when we are so involved in something we lose track of time, are unaware of fatigue and of everything else but the activity itself (think of kids and video games, adults and a gripping novel). His analysis of over 7000 individuals found that the flow experience:

> usually happens when there are clear goals and when the person receives immediate and unambiguous feedback on the activity. Clear goals and feedback are readily available in most games and sports and in many artistic and religious performances, which is the reason such experiences readily provide flow and are intrinsically motivating. *In everyday life, and all too often in classrooms, individuals don't really know what the purpose of their activities is, and it takes them a long time to find out how they are doing.*[176]

It focuses on the task rather than the learner (self/ego)

Peter Johnston has commented, 'There's a world of difference between "*good job*" and "*good boy*"', a similar difference to the 'you must be smart at this' and 'you must have worked really hard' of Carol Dweck's research.[177] Why are these small differences seen as so important? The answer is that they send the learner in different directions. 'Good job' focuses on the work, and if there's other feedback, it will be about how to improve it. It also means if the next piece of work is not as good, we can say so – we are comparing the standards of work. Head off in the other direction and 'good boy' is reputational and teacher-dependent. What do I do to preserve my reputation and what happens when the next piece of work isn't as good and I become a disappointment? Carol Dweck has also shown how this 'you're a star' feedback leads to fixed-ability thinking, which may make students look for easier, failure-free routes (remember Ruth in Chapter 3?). Dweck has studied students who were repeatedly told at school that they were brilliant, but found they were no longer top of the heap when they got to university. This often led, particularly in high-achieving girls, to crises about their ability: Had they been wrong all along? Such crises were much less common with students who saw ability as incremental and effort-related.[178]

It gives cues at appropriate levels on how to bridge the gap

It's not just the direction of feedback, towards the task or the self, but also the level at which it's given that matters.[179] So if we simply give *corrective* feedback about what's right and wrong, the response will be at this level. This may be useful at the very start of mastering a topic as we try to get the basics in place. As we become more competent, *process* feedback becomes more effective; we ask the learner to think about how they got a particular answer and suggest what they may need to consider – 'How could this argument be strengthened?' or 'Can you think of a more dramatic ending?'

The next level is that of *self-regulation*, in which the learner creates internal feedback and self-assessment to engage with the feedback – 'Have you used what you know about writing up an experiment?' or 'What would your own judgement be?' Kluger and DeNisi leave the *self-related feedback* out of their levels framework because it is unproductive, diverting energy to ego-related 'reputational' activity.

131

Michael Absolum has provided a useful framework for this, which I have extended.[180] It involves five levels of feedback prompts, moving from pre-empting mistakes to feedback to those who have met the success criteria.

Feedback prompts

	Feedback Prompts	
Level 0	**Pre-emptive**	Teach rather than wait to give feedback on predictable failure
Level 1	**Example prompt** (corrective)	Clarify what the student is attempting to learn by providing concrete examples: 'Here are two ways of doing this . . .'
Level 2	**Scaffolding prompt** (process)	Students still struggling with concepts/ skills are given more structure: 'What do these measurements show us?'
Level 3	**Reminder prompt** (process – self-regulation)	When learning 'almost there' and learners need a reminder to use it. 'Remember that the conclusion must link back to the topic in the opening paragraph'
Level 4	**Provocative prompt**[181] (self-regulation)	When learners have met the success criteria they are encouraged to think further: 'Can you think of another method you could have used?'; 'How would you argue against it rather than for it?'

The expert's task is to judge at which level to offer feedback. Here's a tricky one to practise on, the task being the following:

Describe what lunchtime is like for you on a school day. Be sure to tell about your lunchtime so that someone who has never had lunch with you on a school day can understand where you have lunch and what lunchtime is like.

What would you offer as feedback on this response?

132

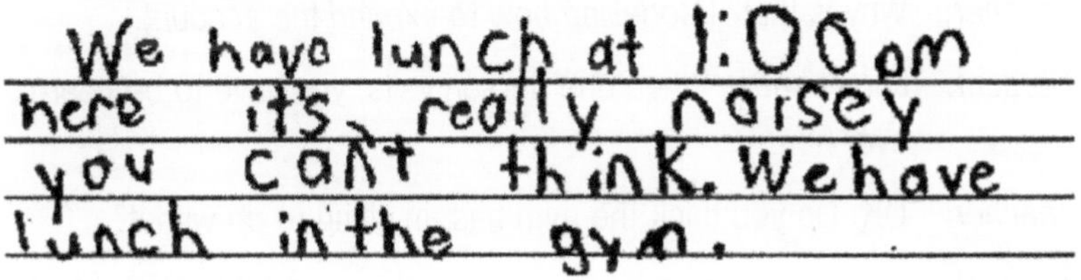

We have lunch at 1:00 pm
here it's really noisey
you can't think. We have
lunch in the gym.

Figure 4 Feedback

In her *How to Give Effective Feedback to Your Students* Susan Brookhart shows how a skilled teacher deals with this.[182] The teacher uses dialogue to scaffold the feedback for this unsuccessful paragraph. A good strategy, given written feedback might be longer than the paragraph itself and count as overwhelming 'killer feedback'.

Teacher: I read your paragraph. Sounds like you really hate lunchtime. [*An honest reader response, showing the student that the teacher has heard what she is saying.*]

Student: Yeah.

Teacher: Is that why this paragraph isn't as good as what you usually write? [*Self-referenced feedback, task focused.*]

Student: Yeah, I hate lunchtime. I didn't want to write about it.

Teacher: Is the noise the worst part? [*Key feature for student, so start there.*]

Student: Yeah.

Teacher: Can you tell me about it? [*Inviting student to say more about the noise.*]

Student: You can't think. The kids are always yelling, and the teachers yell too.

133

Teacher: Why is that? [*Modelling how to expand the account.*]

Student: I don't know. When one person yells, you have to be heard over him.

Teacher: OK. Do you think the gym has anything to do with it?

Student: Yeah. The gym is a big room, so there are lots of kids. And everything echoes.

Teacher: You just told me more about the noisy lunchtime than you put in your paragraph. Would you like to rewrite your paragraph to add some of the points to it? [*This comment 'names for the student the process of identifying details. It offers the next step that should result in improvement'.*]

It is effectively timed

The timing of feedback is a Goldilocks moment. It can be too soon, too late and is hard to get 'just right'. As a general rule it is best done informally, and orally, during the production of work rather than after the work is completed. The contrast here is between a medical diagnosis and a post-mortem; we can do something about a diagnosis. My own rule of thumb would be to try to build in a 'first draft' of any substantial piece of work and focus the feedback on this. As soon as we have to give grades and marks there's plenty of evidence to show feedback will be largely ignored.[183] If we are working with novices, we may need to give fairly rapid corrective feedback to get them on track. This was what John Wooden was doing with his rapid feedback. However, we can be too quick with feedback. What of helpful colleagues and friends who give you the answers to puzzles or crossword clues before you've had time to think? How helpful is it to interrupt a reader while they are in the middle of reading a sentence, or a musician halfway through a line of music? Judy, one of Csikszentmihalyi's talented musical teenagers, testily commented, 'I hate it when they have to ruin the whole challenge for me by stopping me, saying "Stop", trying to show me something.'[184] For her, this was rude, the musical equivalent of 'shut up'. As we saw in Chapter 3, if students are engaged and self-motivated we should leave them until they want feedback; no jumping in and 'rescuing' them, something that may well reduce their involvement.

It is specific and clear

The reason much of our feedback is ineffective is that it is too vague; it provides no information that will help close the gap between where the learner is and where the learner is trying to get to. You have just been unsuccessful in an interview; let me offer you some feedback for next time: 'interview better'. This is unhelpful enough to reduce performance, but it's what we hand out much of the time. Who has not written one of the following?

Good/Study diagram/Very poor/Keep trying harder/Please try harder to improve spelling and neatness/If you need help, ask/Concentrate 100% – check words.

These comments were all taken from a 12-year-old's exercise book in one subject, and there were plenty more like them. Even if the student had wanted to improve, where's the information to work with? How do I improve my spelling? Even feedback like 'explain the science' may seem clear to the teacher, but which part of the science? The refrain here has to be 'Where's the information?'

Good sports coaching offers us a model here. The expert sports coach will give specific feedback that contains the information needed to make improvements.

> "The expert sports coach will give specific feedback that contains the information needed to make improvements."

Norwegians think of cross-country skiing as 'proper' skiing, so when I announced in Norway that I was a novice cross-country skier (because downhill skiing uses techniques that interfere with it), my hosts in Hamar arranged for an expert to work with me. The expert turned out to be Hilde G. Pedersen, World Championship winner and one of Norway's greatest-ever skiers. All a bit intimidating except, as an expert, she simply focused on a couple of basics, balance and rhythm, and the feedback was specifically about these. Even learning how to get up after repeated falls was left till next time – they just picked me up. My hosts' introduction to my talk on expertise the next day was a slideshow of various 'novice' positions.[185]

To be helpful, feedback has to be clear to the recipient. This involves not only the language we use but how clear our communication is. We may use teacherly language our students don't understand or could easily misunderstand: 'illustrate your argument'. So 'give your graph a title' could lead to 'Graph 1' – what Geoff Petty calls 'a failure of intent', with the response 'that's not what I meant'.[186]

Less recognized is that our feedback may be unclear *because our students can't read it.* I worked with a secondary school on their feedback and calculated that at least a quarter of the feedback was illegible, including one comment I deciphered as 'continue to improve your handwriting and spelling'. Students are highly unlikely to approach teachers to ask what an illegible word is, not being able to read it becomes the teacher's problem and the students can ignore it.

It offers strategies rather than solutions

Any feedback that just gives the correct answer, without explaining why, is just about guaranteed to set learning back. If we are told the answer, but not *why* it's the answer, we are put in a worse position than not knowing it at all. This is the importance of the *process* and *self-regulation* levels of feedback; both encourage thinking about how we get to an answer. Yet we often try to nudge students towards a correct answer – 'keep going up' – without checking whether they know why it was right. Dylan Wiliam has provided a good example of moving feedback from solutions to strategies, the corrective level to the process level. You have 20 maths problems with right/wrong answers. Rather than just displaying 15 ticks and 5 crosses he suggests we say to the student, 'Five of these problems are wrong – which are they?'[187]

It challenges, requires action and is achievable

If the purpose of feedback is to make us think, then it must offer some cognitive challenge. 'Well done' and 'poor work' offer us no such challenge. Geoff Petty has framed challenge in terms of 'medals and mission',[188] Shirley Clarke in terms of 'three stars and a wish'.[189] The principle is the same; recognition of what has been done well and then prompts for improvement. Petty points out that high achievers often receive medals and no mission ('excellent!'), while lower achievers get missions and no medals ('you should have . . .'). The lack of recognition of anything done well means they may decide that the goal is unattainable. Remember getting back essays with 'so much teacher red ink on them that the first response was 'I'm no good at this'? As one young pupil hauntingly put it, 'My work is bleeding.' In one school I worked with an art department that seemed to me to pitch feedback perfectly, picking out the positives and then focusing on a specific improvement. Here are just a couple of examples:

> This is a sensitive, well-planned drawing, your lines are light and you have observed carefully. To develop draw a little larger which will assist with achieving a more accurate shape.

Lovely drawing – big and bold. Keep pencil really sharp so edges are hard and crisp.

My guess is that these skilled and specific comments are just the sort that will be responded to by the learners and 'feed forward' into their future work – a case of capacity change.

If we give feedback and then give no opportunity to do anything about it, we have probably wasted our time. This is the problem with feedback at the end of a topic or assignment: it's too late and we have moved on to something else. The task then is to allow time for a response or to build in an opportunity in future work to show it has been addressed. Some teachers put the feedback on a stick-it note or at the back of the exercise book and students can then show when they have subsequently applied it.

So in our feedback we are looking for what sports coaches call 'the sweet spot', where the demands are in the learning zone and the feedback moves us, without panic, to an improved level of performance.

> ❝In our feedback we are looking for what sports coaches call 'the sweet spot', where the demands are in the learning zone and the feedback moves us, without panic, to an improved level of performance.❞

The paradox of praise

Praise the students and make them feel welcomed to your class and worthwhile as learners, but If you wish to make a major difference to learning, leave praise out of feedback about learning.

(John Hattie[190])

We all need praise; it lets us know our efforts are being appreciated and can serve as a motivator. We also know that self-referenced praise can interfere with learning, like the star student who daren't take risks because the result may be less than brilliant. So when we praise, the focus should be on the task and the effort rather than the person. And here's another paradox; expert teachers praise less than other teachers. This is because they expect more, so praise is reserved for efforts over and above what was asked. When I taught in inner London, I would praise students for turning up, bringing a pen and picking up the rubbish they had just dropped. The tiny middle-aged teacher in the next room, who had far fewer discipline problems than I did, never thanked them for bringing pens (and a lot more were 'found' for her lessons) – that was a basic expectation in her classes, as was turning up and never dropping rubbish. If we praise for work that is obviously easy, students may interpret this as us having low estimate of their ability, so praise becomes a negative.[191]

Self-regulated feedback

Getting and giving effective feedback is not the end of the story. Expert learners are able to give themselves feedback that allows them to adjust their performance. We saw in Chapter 2 that one of the key elements in becoming a top-flight musician was the amount of solitary deliberate practice these musicians engaged in. This requires the musician to be monitoring and regulating their performance continuously so that they know what is going well and what needs more work. In a more tangible way top athletes are continuously monitoring their performance: What was my lap time? How do I need to adjust my running/swimming speed? Top cyclists are even more informed. They know their heart rate and what zone they must keep this in as well as the speeds they must maintain.

For our students to become expert learners they will need to assess and adjust their own performance. These are skills that need to be learned and practised. We have looked at the key elements of this in earlier chapters:

being clear about where they are trying to get to; knowing what success looks like; and assessing their current performance. The deliberate practice here is working with exemplars to learn how to make judgements about what quality work looks like. Geoff Petty provides a practical example of learning to give others and oneself feedback.[192]

Learning to give feedback: Snowballing peer assessment to a best answer

- Students arranged in groups of 3 or 4.
- Students given questions or calculations to do – work alone at first (5 min.).
- Students compare answers, reasoning, working etc., noting differences. They discuss and try to agree

    - which are correct or best methods, workings, reasonings and answers and *why*;
    - the group's idea of the 'best answer';
    - what errors were made and *why*.

- Students then given model answers and compare with group answers.
- Class discussion of issues.

This kind of approach takes time to develop, but will repay handsomely as students increasingly become the independent learners we would want them to be. Throughout this book the focus has been on how and why we can encourage learners to think for themselves. In the final chapter we look at how schools and their leaders can contribute to this.

Questions for discussion

1. What has been your own experience of feedback? What can be learned from this in working with students and other teachers?

2. Consider some examples of feedback from students that modified your teaching practices.

3. Take a couple of students' exercise books and review the written feedback you or others have given. How much of it is informative and specific enough to move learning forward?

4. Develop a classroom activity that can help students to develop self-regulated feedback.

7

The Expert School

If I ran a school, I'd give the average grade to the ones who gave me all the right answers, for being good parrots. I'd give the top grades to those who made a lot of mistakes and told me about them, and then told me what they learned from them.

(R. Buckminster Fuller[193])

Buckminster Fuller, architect (he of the geodesic dome) and inventor. said this way back in the twentieth century. His point is a powerful one, if oversimplified. Gary Klein nuances it by pointing out that:

When we are skilled, we can learn more from failures than successes. When we are beginning to acquire skills, positive examples that we can model may be more helpful. That is because when we are starting we have no shortages of failures but lack the sophisticated mental models to learn from them. When we are skilled, failures are less frequent and highly instructive. They let us find the flaws in our mental models.[194]

This sits well with the messages of this book about the need to develop mental models, the importance of modelling and of learning from failure.

So if we're serious about the fabled twenty-first-century learner, that flexible, cooperative, analytic and self-regulating student, we're going to have to change our ways.

This won't be easy. As in many countries, this will mean battling the policy headwinds, which, in their PISA panic, are encouraging instrumental learning and ever greater teacher dependence. There will also be unhelpful cultural currents, for example, those driven in the UK by the legacy of beliefs about innate ability. This still dogs us in the form of pressures for early streaming, the way we interpret ability test results and our thinking about 'gifted and talented' students. There are other wider cultural legacies to contend with too: the assumption that teaching is about 'teachers talking and learners listening' and that 'real work' in the classroom must involve writing – even though it rarely does so in the outside world.

> "If we're serious about the fabled twenty-first-century learner, that flexible, cooperative, analytic and self-regulating student, we're going to have to change our ways."

The expert school – having its own vision

So the expert school will need to be brave and to do things differently. This will mean having its own values and philosophy that will help resist what Michael Gunzenhauser has called *the default philosophy of education*, which 'places inordinate value on the scores achieved on high-stakes tests, rather than on the achievement that the scores are meant to represent'.[195] Because of the power of this default philosophy, teachers in the current climate 'may find themselves doing things that fall short of their visions of themselves as educators, such as drilling students on practice tests, deemphasizing or elimination of untested subject matter, or teaching to the test'.[196] This was

143

something Mary James and colleagues found in their *Learning How to Learn* project, that teachers were involved in practices that were a long way from their ideals.[197] This also means that school leadership needs courage to stand up for a better vision of learning. There's been plenty of good writing on this, including Michael Fullan and Andy Hargreaves's nattily titled *What's Worth Fighting for in Your School*,[198] so I'll hand the baton over to them.

This chapter heads for new horizons by drawing together what we've learned about expertise and its application to classroom learning. It calls for radical thinking, but not in the sense of tearing everything up and starting again. We have the same schools, the same teachers and students but some different thinking about how we learn and how we teach. I group this thinking around four main expertise themes: *opportunities, high demands, deliberate practice and reflective learning*.

Expertise needs opportunities

The argument throughout this book has been that expertise is developed, not inborn. We become experts as a result of the opportunities we are offered and how we interact with them. So if I ask you what you are good at, and how and why you got good, what would your answer be? For many it would be about professional expertise, something that has developed with opportunity and experience. For others it may be a sport, or music or other hobbies. Here the interest may have been sparked by family, as often the case in music, or by opportunities outside school. We saw that for Jessica Ennis this was a local athletics camp, for the Brontës it was writing with siblings, for the Polgar sisters it was their father's beliefs about learning, as it was for Mozart. Matthew Syed's 'child prodigies do not have unusual genes; they have unusual upbringings' captures this nicely.[199] A good example of this is the diminutive double Olympic gold-medal-winning cyclist Laura Trott. She was born prematurely with a collapsed lung and

144

later developed asthma (no 'born cyclist' then). As a child she and her family took up cycling, in part because of medical advice to build up her lungs. This provided the spark and she became increasingly committed, so that by age 20 she was world and Olympic champion.[200]

Opportunity comes in all shapes and sizes. For the Z-Boys, who revolutionized skateboarding into the acrobatic form it is today, it was swimming-pool shaped. These youth were surfing bums who, when there was no surf, skateboarded. Ever pushing their limits they found that empty swimming pools, of which there were many in Bel Air and Beverley Hills thanks to 'drought, fire and overbuilt real estate',[201] provided the opportunity for developing moves never before attempted.

For Desmond Douglas, Britain's greatest-ever table-tennis player, opportunity came in the form of a table-tennis table wedged into a small classroom in his school. The room was so small he had to stand right up against the table and react extremely quickly, so he and his classmates had to play 'speed table tennis' rather than drop back from the table and use spins and other strategies. Douglas was known as 'lightning man' and it was assumed he had inherited very fast reflexes. However, when his reactions were tested they were the slowest in the England team, slower even than the junior, cadets and the team manager.[202] So his anticipation and reactions had been developed by five years of practice on an 'impossible' table with one of his classmates commenting, 'he spent all his time in that classroom practising his skills and playing matches. I have never seen anyone with such dedication.'[203]

These examples illustrate how opportunity is not so much about high-quality resources as about the chance for playful, deliberate practice. How many schools decide that they don't have space for a table-tennis table or a non-supervised chess club or a music practice room? We saw earlier how Bill Gates's interest in computing was sparked by the introduction of a computer room in his school, with privileged access to real-time programming. Steve Redgrave's introduction to rowing was in

145

boats borrowed from local clubs by his English teacher. For many years the *Times Educational Supplement* (*TES*) in England ran a column *My Best Teacher*,[204] in which celebrities identified and talked about a teacher who had been important to their development. There are common themes, which mirror those found by Bloom and Csikszentmihalyi, that run through these accounts. Best teachers:

- were passionate about what they taught;
- saw something in students that other teachers often didn't;
- encouraged them and provided opportunities to progress.

So, for example, it was the enthusiasm of his teacher for literature that 'was infectious' for novelist Ian Rankin, as was the art teacher of TV series *Hairy Bikers*' Dave Myers, who 'taught me to be myself and to be enthusiastic'. It was these teachers who made subjects interesting, even for students who had little interest in school. The actor Peter Duncan failed his 11+ selection exam and found secondary modern school 'dull compared with my life outside', except for his history teacher whose 'dynamic debates and exciting discussions shone out. He managed to bring about a mind shift in us dogged children.' Sarah Beeney, the TV property developer, who 'hated school pretty much right through . . . and didn't see the point of half the stuff I was being taught at school', benefited from an English teacher who 'Rather than tell me what to do, . . . suggested what might be a good idea . . . [and] encouraged me in directions in which I was interested, which I think is the sign of a clever teacher.'

Perhaps the strongest message from these accounts was that these teachers recognized potential in the students. For chef Antony Worrall Thompson, it was his maths teacher who was the only one this troubled adolescent could turn to, and who believed him when he reported that another teacher was abusing boys. The maths teacher acted on this information and

146

the other teacher was sacked. For singer-songwriter Beverley Knight, 'one of six black kids in a school of 400-plus', it was her teacher from primary school who told her that she 'was very special and would achieve whatever I wanted in life'. Black theologian Robert Beckford went to an inner city comprehensive school where 'expectations for black children were very low ... I was encouraged to do sport like all the other black kids', and was good enough to sign for Wolverhampton Wanderers football team at age 14. It was a politically radical 'science-cum-computer science teacher' who got him to question why black students were overrepresented in sports teams and underrepresented in the academic clubs and the higher groups of maths, English and science. He also gave him a copy of *The Autobiography of Malcolm X* when he was 14 and 'that was a turning point. . . . Until that teacher came along I had been in the lower groups and frequented ESN classes.'[205] He got serious about learning at this point, a process leading to his PhD.

One of the most powerful examples of teacher support is that of David Blunkett, a former Education Secretary in the UK's Labour government. Born blind, he attended a special school but was not satisfied with the low academic expectations, so he went to the local technical college to do his O and A level studies.[206] This was 'a long haul' for a blind student. It took him three years to get six O levels and he was 22 by the time he got all his qualifications for university. What made this transition possible was a teacher who gave up one night a week to act as his mentor and support worker at the college. David Blunkett nominated this teacher 'not because he was the world's best teacher but because he was the most dedicated and supportive . . . I'd have floundered without him'.

Opportunities for all

So far I have largely focused on opportunities afforded to individuals. Every school will be able to point to a few, or many, individuals who have gone on to show high levels of performance and for whom school played an important role. But the expert school needs to offer all its students a chance to be expert learners, and its teachers the encouragement to become expert teachers. So the question becomes 'How do we offer opportunities for students and teachers to become expert learners in day-to-day classroom life?'

A belief that I developed during my work as an educational psychologist is that everyone is good at something – if we can find out what it is. I came across kids who were doing badly in school, who thought they 'knew nuffinck', who in fact knew lots about fishing or pop music or the history of their football team. They just never got asked or invited to base work on them. I also learned that you can never be sure who's going to finish up where – the most well-known, and now richest, student from my old school left to work in a betting shop instead of taking his school leaving exams. None would have predicted fame and fortune for Bill Wyman, who then joined the Rolling Stones.

Less anecdotally, Benjamin Bloom's research into 120 top adult performers concluded that this success could only have been predicted for 10 per cent of these at age 12 or so. And, as Terman found with his 'Termites' (see Chapter 1) few who, on the basis of their IQs, were predicted to do great things, did. One final flurry on this: Thomas Edison was expelled from his primary school because his teacher declared him 'subnormal', while we saw in the last chapter that biology Nobel Laureate John Gurdon was rubbished by his science teacher. While coming bottom of the year in biology he was busy creating his own collection of moths and butterflies. So we need to be careful about the way we label our students and predict their futures. Respect is in order.

The importance of choice

We can't let everyone go off and do their own thing. Most teachers have a curriculum, subjects and classes of 30 to consider. But within these constraints there may be more opportunities for choice than we allow. The motivation literature is clear on this; the more students take ownership of their work, the more they will put into it. Even being asked to make small choices, 'choose one of the three', has an impact on learning. As we saw in Chapter 3, Daniel Pink argues that many successful businesses have moved away from 'carrot and stick' approaches to motivation and have adopted practices that allow workers more autonomy, so that motivation becomes more intrinsic. His maxim is, 'Think autonomy, not control. State the outcome you need. But instead of specifying precisely the way to reach it . . . give them freedom over how they do the job.'[207] His own example is that of workers who have to wrap and send out posters, a job that would beat most lessons in terms of tedium. The traditional approach is to set targets and provide incentives and sanctions, mirroring schools' use of tracking, targets and monitoring. Pink argues that we will get more done, and done better, if we say 'we've got this number of posters to send out; we'll leave you to sort out how you do it'. I can sense mutterings of 'try that with class 8F and see what happens'. Class 8F may well need some help getting to this stage, since 'learned helplessness' may be a reflex as might heavy teacher dependence. So it may need plenty of exemplars, modelling and group work to get this going.

But this is not blue skies territory. This is exactly what the exceptional achievers of both Bloom's and Csikszentmihalyi's research said: they enjoyed learning most when they were allowed to find their own solutions and lost motivation when they simply had to follow the method the teacher had given them.[208] And this was at the heart of creative maths teaching in Stigler and Hiebert's study of Japanese classrooms – set a problem and let the students, working in groups, try to find a solution.[209] The teacher's role is then to show ways forward when they are stuck. If we are serious about the self-regulated twenty-first-century learner, we will need to give more opportunities to choose and more autonomy, even within everyday classroom learning.

Social learning

The biggest anomaly in schooling today is that we know all about the importance of social learning and yet we do so little of it. By social learning I'm focusing on students working together, on collaborative efforts and on classroom discussions. Learning theory supports social learning, as does the research evidence and the student vote.[210] It's also central to the twenty-first-century learner's skills. The problem is that there isn't a lot of it around in classrooms. So the opportunities for learners to find out from others, to test out ideas, to collaborate are minimized. In John Hattie's observational research this kind of group learning occupied less than 5 per cent of classroom time. So the expert school will place much more emphasis on learners working together, like the 'snowballing' lesson in the previous chapter.

Social learning is not something that happens without structure and practice. We need 'rules of engagement': how learners conduct themselves in groups; what teamwork involves. My 'best buy' on this is the work of Neil Mercer and colleagues who have provided plentiful research and practical advice on how we can make groups and group discussions work.[211]

Independent problem solving

We learn well in groups, but we still have to learn for ourselves and some of this will be solitary learning. A common finding across the study of experts and of exceptional students is their capacity to become absorbed and to concentrate for long periods of time on specific tasks. We saw earlier that what distinguished elite musicians from others was the extent of their solitary deliberate practice. Bloom's study of scientists and neurologists found that when they were children, they would often spend time by themselves making models and assembling kits, solving problems they set themselves. Buckminster Fuller, who introduced this chapter, could not grasp the abstractions of geometry as a child but was constantly collecting and making models and inventions from natural materials.

This capacity to concentrate is not just the preserve of future scientists and musicians. Even in 8F there will be students who will be absorbed for hours at a time with computer games, pop music and sports. Watching adolescents practise their skateboarding for hours at a time, risky practice too – very little of it in the comfort zone – I recognize these same adolescents as the ones who may give up in a nanosecond if they are given a complex maths problem or written assignment. So how do we bridge the gap between their capacity to concentrate when they want to and the learned helplessness of the classroom? It's partly back to choice (What would they choose to focus on in this topic?), partly down to skilled tuning in by the teacher (What problems can you solve outside school that will help with this?) and adapting the approach (How does this link to the students' interests?).

There's nothing new in this for the experienced teacher. It's another case of our knowing something but making limited use of it in the classroom. In England many teachers of English will be familiar with Barry Hines's *A Kestrel for a Knave* and/or Ken Loach's film *Kes*. This captures perfectly the points being made here, a poor student from a deprived family who, according to the Youth Employment Officer, has no interests. Yet he has raised and trained a kestrel and knows all about them. Do his teachers find out about this expertise and harness it?

Schools as multipliers

One of the key mechanisms in the development of expertise is the presence of social and individual multipliers, small advantages that give rise to further opportunities that create an upward spiral of success. These will involve expectations, resources and support. Sadly, in the UK, unlike many other countries, some of these multipliers can be bought through the private school system. Though independent schools educate only 7 per cent of the school population, 60 per cent of ministers in the 2010 Cabinet in the UK were privately educated, as were half of the coalition's Members of Parliament. This is even more pronounced in the legal system, with half of England's judges attending boarding schools, which educate less than 1 per cent of the school population. It's a similar story in most top professions.[212] And just to rub salt into the wounds, over half the UK's medallists in the 2008 Olympics were privately educated, a percentage described by Lord Moynihan, Britain's Olympic Chairman in 2012, as one of 'the worst statistics in British sport . . . there's so much talent out there in the 93 per cent that should be identified and developed'.[213] The figure dropped to 32 per cent in the 2012 Olympics, an improvement credited to intervention programmes, so that in rowing 50 per cent of the rowing teams were from state schools as opposed to the overwhelmingly privately educated 2008 teams. This is good news, tempered perhaps by the knowledge that the Olympic rowing venue, Dorney Lake, is privately owned by Eton College, which had it developed at a cost of £17 million.

But, as you may have deduced, my involvement is with the 93 per cent and how we offer opportunities with fewer resources and less staff time. My reading of the situation is that schools *are* seeking to provide multipliers, with many teachers going 'above and beyond' their contractual duties. The *My Best Teacher* column provides a litany of teachers willing to put on school plays, concerts, school trips that triggered interest in history and geography. We could take this a step further so that schools conduct an audit of the opportunities they offer around and beyond the classroom.

This would include an informal inventory of the outside interests of every student; informal because it would be the result of teachers getting alongside their students to talk about them, rather than having to make up an answer for a survey. What is the match between what is offered and what students are interested in and what can be done to improve it? Would we know if one of our quiet students was raising a kestrel, writing poems or looking after a sick grandmother?

Expert schools make high demands

Children grow into the intellectual life of those around them.

(Vygotsky[214])

We know that experts set themselves demanding goals and that deliberate practice involves leaving the comfort zone. Sports coaches talk about the 'sweet spot', the demand that has about a 50/50 chance of success, attainable but with an equal chance of initial failure. We saw in Chapter 3 that the main difference between expert and experienced teachers is in making deeper demands of their students, who then have to think for themselves. Expert schools provide a culture in which this will happen. This in turn means that leaders and classroom teachers have to model this in their own professional learning. This is the main thrust of Andy Hargreaves and Michael Fullan's *Professional Capital: Transforming Teaching in Every School*. A central argument in this is that teachers have to move beyond being 'enthusiastic amateurs':

> but in the end, if you don't know the difference between good and bad teaching, if you aren't aware of the strategies that succeed with students and haven't learned how to use them, if you do things for fun but that don't really get students to learn more, then you will

> "Even with the best of intentions, even if you seem like a 'natural' as a teacher, unless you deliberately learn how to get better so you can teach the students of today for the world of tomorrow, you will not be teaching like a pro. You will just be an enthusiastic amateur."
> – Andy Hargreaves and Michael Fullan

sell your students short. Even with the best of intentions, even if you seem like a 'natural' as a teacher, unless you deliberately learn how to get better so you can teach the students of today for the world of tomorrow, you will not be teaching like a pro. You will just be an enthusiastic amateur.[215]

A footnote to this is Stigler and Hiebert's observation that education policy tends to focus more on the quality of teachers, who we get, rather than on the quality of teaching, what they do. They point out that even the brightest and best will soon fall into line with the culture of the school:

Teachers follow scripts that they acquire as members of their culture, and their effectiveness depends on the scripts they use. Recruiting highly qualified teachers will not result in steady improvement as long as they use the same scripts. It's the scripts that must be improved.[216]

It was the scripts about how we learn, diagnostics, clarity about learning and feedback that the previous four chapters have sought to improve.

High demands are not just for high achievers

A legacy of Anglo-Saxon ability myths is the assumption that many children cannot cope with 'academic' demands. Historically these assumptions have been largely class-related and reflected in the divide between the grammar and secondary modern, with the 11+ exam as the means of sifting. We saw in Chapter 1 how the achievements of high-scoring infants from low socioeconomic groups (SES) actually decline once they start school, while those of low-scoring high-SES infants steadily improve. This is about expectations and opportunities.

So good readers use the same patterns of reading skills acquisition as weaker readers, but there are often massive differences in exposure to books[217] – just as there may have been to spoken words (p.63). As soon as we make fixed-ability assumptions, we are likely to restrict our demands on the low ability and create a self-fulfilling script. This is the *Matthew effect* (after Matthew 25:29) in which, to paraphrase, 'the rich get richer and the poor get poorer'. Using the example of reading, Keith Stanovich points out that early success in learning to read is a multiplier, leading to more reading and broader educational success since other cognitive processes track the level of reading skill. Those struggling with reading will read less and the gap between them and their peers will widen as 'learning to read' transmutes into 'reading to learn'.[218] This we all know from experience; the issue is whether we settle for it or seek to close the gap. Maths has similar multipliers – here's a comment from a bottom maths set student:

Sir treats us like we're babies, puts us down, makes us copy stuff off the board, puts up all the answers like we don't know anything.

And we're not going to learn from that, 'cause we've got to think for ourselves.[219]

> "Schools with high expectations do not write off low achievers; they too must think for themselves."

Schools with high expectations do not write off low achievers; they too must think for themselves.

Playfulness

To be playful and serious at the same time . . . defines the ideal mental condition.

(John Dewey[220])

Making high demands does not mean making life unpleasant for students, turning schools into educational boot camps. A paradox of expert learning is the rigours of deliberate practice are often enjoyed, especially when coaches and teachers are imaginative. So Laszlo Polgar made learning chess an enjoyable activity for his three daughters, while Serena and Venus Williams's father made up all sorts of training games. In Bloom's study of exceptional musicians the early learning phases were all construed as fun: 'tinkering around' and 'tapping out melodies', with music lessons seen as a pleasure. The only exception was a child who was sent to lessons because his parents thought it was 'a good thing'. Lessons were disliked and ducked, and progress was minimal. They were just about to be abandoned when he heard a recording of piece of piano music at school, which he suddenly wanted to be able to play himself – even though it was way too difficult. It was during this stage of struggling with a difficult piece (Grieg) that for the first time lessons became enjoyable: 'I think it was play time. It was fun time. I'd just play my pieces. I'd play them badly. She'd make suggestions. I'd try them again.'[221]

This fits well with Csikszentmihalyi's findings:

Teachers can achieve their educational objectives best by focusing their efforts on making learning enjoyable . . . motivation . . . has to do with the active enjoyment of learning

> "Teachers can achieve their educational objectives best by focusing their efforts on making learning enjoyable . . . motivation . . . has to do with the active enjoyment of learning to ride a bike or to swim or to solve a difficult puzzle or build a table." – Mihali Csikszentmihalyi

156

to ride a bike or to swim or to solve a difficult puzzle or build a table. In other words, intrinsically rewarding learning produces an experience of growth and of mastery, a feeling that the person has succeeded in expanding her or his skills.[222]

Making learning a problem

What comes through loud and clear from the previous quotation, as well as the expertise literature and studies of exceptional students, is that we learn best when we are searching for a personal solution. That was what the Japanese maths teaching culture that Stigler and Hiebert investigated had developed – set the students a problem and provide information and instruction when necessary. This was what both Bloom's and Csikszentmihalyi's students reported, they enjoyed finding their own solutions and disliked having simply to follow the teacher's procedures. We learned from Chapter 3 that good diagnostics involve open-ended questions that assess the students' own ideas.

In many occupations, particularly in medicine and business, *problem-based learning* is a core teaching method. So, for example, many of the business, law and medical courses at Harvard operate on this principle. While there are many variations, the basic processes are that groups of students are presented with scenarios and have to use the information, and other information that may subsequently be drip-fed to them or they find for themselves, to arrive at a conclusion or decision. It is not difficult to see how this presses all the twenty-first-century learner buttons. The challenge is to move this into schools.

We will still need to teach. Problem-based approaches are about providing the tools but then asking students to use them creatively rather than simply following a script. And as they get better, the problems become more subtle. So I'm not advocating a form of 'discovery' learning in which students are expected to find out unaided. Discovery is about making sense of information and techniques for yourself. The Japanese maths teachers always linked their new problem to what had gone in previous lessons ('tuning in') so there were both cues and learned techniques to draw on. The New Zealand primary numeracy strategy requires pupils to think of two ways in which a problem might be solved before they start any computation. The result is that these pupils are more flexible when presented with a new problem, while conventionally trained pupils tend to use lengthy rule-based procedures, even when there are much more efficient solutions. 97 + 53 is a doddle if you're flexible.

Keeping practice purposeful

Most of the practice we do in our everyday lives maintains, rather than improves, what we can do. We do not get into our cars and say, 'Today I'm going to improve my gear changing.' The same may be true of our teaching. *Deliberate practice* is purposeful in that it seeks to improve performance by focusing on specific elements. For Anders Ericsson the most effective learning:

> requires a well-defined task with an appropriate difficulty level for the particular individual, informative feedback, and opportunities for repetition and correction of errors. When all these elements are present . . . *deliberate practice* [characterizes] training activities.[223]

Less of the same

We would often say we meet those conditions in the classroom. We introduce a new topic and provide examples to work on. That's fine, as long as the examples are not the equivalent of 20 similar items so that the difficulty level drops back into the comfort zone once the first item is mastered. This takes us back to Howard Gardner's plea:

> You've got to take enough time to get kids deeply involved in something so they can think about it in lots of different ways and apply it – not just at school but at home and on the street and so on.[224]

So deliberate practice has to be very deliberate: better to set five problems coming at the same learning from different angles than 20 'more of the same' ones. We saw in Chapter 2 that expert scientists, when faced with a new problem, home in on the scientific principles involved, while novices attend to the surface features. So for the novice every new problem really is a new problem; for the expert it is usually just a variation on a theme.

This is not just an issue for individual teachers, the culture of a school determines the kinds of practice teachers require of their students. Homework policy is an example of this. How much of this encourages volume of work rather than the quality of work? Is the culture one of answering textbook questions rather than applying newly learned principles to everyday problems?

> "The culture of a school determines the kinds of practice teachers require of their students. Homework policy is an example of this."

Risk taking and failure

In his radical 1960s *How Children Fail*, John Holt rails at how we dampen curiosity in schools: 'Nobody starts off stupid. You have only to watch babies and infants and think seriously about what all of them learn or do.'[225] The problem, for him, is that we adults destroy this intellectual curiosity by making them 'afraid of not pleasing, of making mistakes,

> **"Novices need to experience success; that's what encourages deeper engagement, and the more this is the outcome of thinking for themselves, the more powerful a multiplier it will be."**

of failing, of being *wrong* . . . so that by the age of ten most of them will not ask questions'. In this book I have looked at how we can encourage learning risks in the classroom, how we move into the learning zone and look for that 50/50 'sweet spot'. Novices need to experience success; that's what encourages deeper engagement, and the more this is the outcome of thinking for themselves, the more powerful a multiplier it will be.

So the expert school has to encourage a culture in which we are expected to take learning risks. This starts with the leaders, who model it for teachers, who model it for students. Daring school leaders, for example, send out the message that they do the following:

- support learning in depth even though that may mean less coverage;
- want teachers to get well beyond 5 per cent of lesson time being spent in group learning;
- would welcome more time being spent in classroom dialogue and rich questioning;
- encourage teachers to conduct at least one 'risky' lesson a week, which involves doing something new for which the outcome is not assured;
- support teachers who want to do things differently for reasons they can justify;
- encourage collaboration in researching new lessons on difficult topics.

When school leaders are modelling learning (What are you currently learning outside school?) and risk taking, we can then ask our students to take risks in their learning.

A vital part of this is a culture in which getting something wrong is seen as productive rather than a humiliation.

Here's some modelling of being prepared to fail. The selective Wimbledon High School for Girls is full of academically successful girls who achieve top grades in national exams. As we saw earlier this can lead to avoidance of failure: reputations as top students have to be maintained. To make the point that failure is a key part of success, the headteacher organized a 'failure week' in which speakers, teachers and parents discussed with students the importance of risk taking and what can be learned from failure. Her message was as follows:

> My message to girls is that it is better to lead a life replete with disappointment than one in which you constantly wonder 'if only' . . . For high achieving girls in particular, where fear of failure can be crippling, this is vitally important.[226]

And in the box below are some thoughts for a wall poster that learning involves risk and failure. I'm sure you could add more.

Better to try and fail than never try

I've missed more than 9000 shots in my career. I've lost almost 300 games. 26 times, I've been trusted to take the game winning shot and missed. I've failed over and over and over again in my life. And that is why I succeed.
Basketball superstar Michael Jordan's *Nike* advert

By any conventional measure, a mere seven years after my graduation day I had failed on an epic scale . . . I am not going to stand here and tell you failure is fun.

J.K. Rowling

(whose first Harry Potter story was rejected by 12 publishers)

Success consists of going from failure to failure without loss of enthusiasm.

Sir Winston Churchill

Many of life's failures are people who did not realize how close they were to success when they gave up.

Thomas Edison

Becoming expert learners

Experts have responded to the opportunities with which they have been presented and developed the motivation to succeed. They put themselves through often gruelling practice schedules, though paradoxically they see this deliberate practice as a source of engagement and pleasure. Their development has often been encouraged by multipliers that bring success and further opportunities. Expert teaching, coaching and mentoring are essential parts of this process as learners are apprenticed to experts whose mental frameworks allow them to see 'the big picture'. This involves a clear sense of learning progression and providing regular and effective feedback. This in turn leads to

162

self-monitoring skills, which allow experts to assess and regulate their own performance.

This book has sought to translate our knowledge about expert learning into everyday educational practices. The intention is not to hothouse geniuses but rather find ways for all learners to mirror these processes so that they learn to think for themselves and are confident that they can tackle new learning situations – 'knowing what to do when you don't know what to do'. This means, in cultures like the UK, challenging assumptions about fixed ability and how talent is rationed. It also means resisting instrumentalist pressures to focus simply on results. We want good results, but based on good understanding rather than rote learning and drilling.

If we are to produce expert learners, we need expert teachers and leaders. Students learn by modelling what they are exposed to. If they are not encouraged to think and question for themselves, they will not do it. If schools do not offer opportunities that develop students' interests, their learning in school will be impoverished. As Andy Hargreaves and Michael Fullan have argued, teachers have to develop their expertise to do this.[227] Being an enthusiastic amateur is not enough. To 'teach like a pro' we need to have the same professional discipline as other experts; we need to develop our mental frameworks and deliberately practise skills of leadership and teaching.

And if our students are to be expert learners, they must be able to monitor their learning. For this they need demanding, but attainable, goals that will require them to think for themselves, to 'make sense' of what they are learning. Motivation comes when they become engaged in such learning, for example, the pleasure that the high-achieving maths and science students got from developing their *own* solutions to problems. This is best when high demands and playfulness are combined. We can give all students the tools for expert learning by helping them understand the why and how of learning something through tuning in, clear learning intentions and modelling success. And when learners are clear about these, they can begin to evaluate their current performance, the start of reflecting on their own work and that of others.

We also know that experts have received effective feedback as one of the key multipliers in their development. Skilled sports coaches have a clear sense of progression and a wide repertoire of practice drills from which they can select the most appropriate one for an individual. In the classroom, specific, task-focused and timely feedback mirrors this, with students increasingly able to judge the quality of their own performance. When learners are able to monitor and regulate the quality of their own work, we have the beginnings of real expertise.

The Expanding Educational Horizons series encourages educators to look beyond the immediate pressures and practices of their work. This book is a reminder of how expert learning develops. John Dewey saw this horizon over 80 years ago – so I'll leave him with the final word:

> We state emphatically that, upon its intellectual side education consists in the formation of wide-awake, careful, thorough habits of thinking. Of course intellectual learning includes the amassing and retention of information. But information is an undigested burden unless it is understood. It is knowledge only as material is comprehended. And understanding, comprehension, means that the various parts of the information are grasped in their relations to one another – a result that is attained only when acquisition is accompanied by constant reflection upon the meaning of what is studied.[228]

'Are we there yet?'

Questions for discussion

1. Does our school/college/organization have a clear vision of its own? What elements of 'default philosophy' has this allowed us to resist?

2. How do we find out our students' interests and what opportunities do we offer them, particularly our lower-achieving students, to develop these?

3. What is the dominant script for teachers in our school in relation to student choice, social learning and independent problem solving?

4. How enjoyable/playful is learning made for our students?

5. How effectively are our school leaders and teachers modelling expert learning?

Notes

Introduction

1 I mainly use *student* in this book to cover learners of all ages. This may not sit comfortably for some readers as in England *pupil* is often used for younger children (up to 14 years) and student for older ones. European countries tend to use the word pupil for all school age children, and North America, Australia and New Zealand use student – so there's no neat solution.

2 Attributed to Piaget. John Holt (1982) makes a similar point in his *How Children Fail*, London: Penguin Books: 'The true test of intelligence is not how much we know how to do, but how we behave when we don't know what to do' (p.271).

3 See Ericsson, K.A., Charness, N., Feltovich, P.J. and Hoffman, R. R. (eds) (2006) *The Cambridge Handbook of Expertise and Expert Performance.* Cambridge: Cambridge University Press.

4 Gladwell, M. (2008) *Outliers: The Story of Success.* London: Allen Lane.

5 Syed, M. (2010) *Bounce: How Champions Are Made.* London: Fourth Estate.

6 See Chi, M.T.H. (2006) Two approaches to the study of experts' characteristics, in Ericsson et al., pp. 23–4. See note 3.

7 Syed, 2010 (p.59). See note 5.

8 For example, Ericsson, K.A., Krampe, R.T. and Tesch-Romer, C. (1993) The role of deliberate practice in the acquisition of expert performance, *Psychological Review*, 100: 364–403.

9 Beckham, D. (2010) *My Side.* EPUB edn, HarperCollins e-books. The three quotations are from pp. 111–15, 138–40 and 172–7.

10 Daniel Taylor (2013) David Beckham exits as gracefully as one of his arcing crosses, *Guardian* D, 16 May. Available at http://www.guardian.co.uk/football/blog/2013/may/16/david-beckham-retires-career [Accessed 16 May 2013].
11 Syed, 2010 (pp. 21–2). See note 5.
12 Howe, M.J.A. (1999) *Genius Explained*, pp. 2–7. Cambridge: Cambridge University Press.
13 See Chapter 13 in McGrayne, S.B. (2002) *Nobel Prize Women in Science*. Washington: Joseph Henry Press.
14 Syed, 2010 (p.5). See note 5.
15 Coyle, D. (2010) *The Talent Code*, p.65. London: Arrow Books.
16 Ennis, J. (2012) *Unbelievable: From My Childhood Dreams to Winning Olympic Gold*. London: Hodder and Stoughton.
17 Hart, S., Dixon, A., Drummond, M.J. and McIntyre, D. (2004) *Learning Without Limits*, p.21. Maidenhead: Open University Press.
18 Lucas, B. and Claxton, G. (2010) *New Kinds of Smart: How the Science of Learnable Intelligence Is Changing Education*. Maidenhead: Open University Press McGraw-Hill.
19 The familiar names here would be those of James Watson and Ivan Pavlov.
20 See Gladwell, 2008, Chapter 1, for the first two questions. See note 4.
21 For the last two questions, see Crawford, C., Dearden, L. and Greaves, E. (2011) *Does When You Are Born Matter? The Impact of Month of Birth on Children's Cognitive and Non-Cognitive Skills in England*. London: Institute for Fiscal Studies.
22 Klein, G. (1999) *Sources of Power*. Cambridge, MA: MIT Press.
23 Assessment Reform Group (2002) *Assessment for Learning: 10 Principles*. Cambridge: University of Cambridge, Assessment Reform Group.

Chapter 1: Nothing's Fixed: Tackling Ability Myths

24 Sternberg, R.J. (1999) Intelligence as developing expertise, *Contemporary Educational Psychology*, 24(4): 359–75.
25 See, for example, Hursh, D. (2005) The growth of high-stakes testing in the USA: accountability, markets and the decline of educational equality, *British Educational Research Journal*, 31: 605–22.
26 Gillborn, D. and Youdell, D. (2001) The new IQism: intelligence, 'ability' and the rationing of education, in J. Demaine (ed.) *Sociology of Education Today* (p.81). Basingstoke: Palgrave (their italics).
27 For a more detailed treatment, see Stobart, G. (2008) *Testing Times*. Abingdon: Routledge, Chapters 2–4.

28   Broadfoot, P. (1979) *Assessment, Schools and Society*, p.44. London: Methuen.
29   Burt, C.L.S. (1959) The examination at eleven plus, *British Journal of Educational Studies*, 7: 114.
30   Burt, C.L.S. (1937) *The Backward Child*, pp. 10–11. London: University of London Press.
31   Binet, A. (1909) *Les Idées Modernes sur les Enfants*, pp. 100–1. Paris: Flammarion.
32   Ibid., p.104.
33   Greulich, W.W. (1997) A comparison of the physical growth and development of American-born and native Japanese children, *American Journal of Physical Anthropology*, 15: 489–515.
34   Turkheimer, E., Haley, A., Waldron, M., D'Onofrio, B. and Gottesman, I. (2003) Socioeconomic status modifies heritability of IQ in young children, *Psychological Science*, 14(6): 623–8.
35   Block, N. (1995) How heritability misleads about race, *Cognition*, 56: 99–128.
36   But there is plenty of this kind of argument around, with researchers even looking for the genetic basis of religious and political beliefs. See, for example, Lewis, G.J. and Bates, T.C. (2013) The long reach of the gene, *Psychologist*, 26(3): 194–8.
37   Michael Rutter makes a powerful argument for this in relation to mental illness. While certain genes are associated with certain illnesses, many people with these genetic patterns don't develop the illnesses, while some without these genetic patterns do. See Rutter, M., Moffitt, T.E. and Caspi, A. (2006) Gene–environment interplay and psychopathology: multiple varieties but real effects, *Journal of Child Psychology and Psychiatry*, 47: 226–61.
38   Plomin, R. and Walker, S.O. (2003) Genetics and educational psychology, *British Journal of Educational Psychology*, 73: 3–14.
39   Gould, S.J. (1996) *The Mismeasure of Man*, p.34. New York: Norton.
40   Burt falsified the original data by counting the same studies several times and then writing up the results using fictitious authors and publishing them in the journal he edited. There have been more recent, and reputable, studies by such as Thomas Bouchard in the US and Robert Plomin in the UK, which claim a strong genetic component, though there is doubt about just how 'separate' the upbringing of these identical twins was.
      However, even in Bouchard's larger study, the average age of the separated twins studied was 40, while they typically had spent 30 years apart, which meant 10 years of contact prior to the interviews (Shenk, D. [2011] *The Genius in All of Us*, p.69. London: Icon Books). Earlier research had looked at 121 twins 'separated at birth' or 'reared apart' and found that only three of those pairs had been separated shortly after birth and studied at their first reunion (Farber, S. [1981], *Identical Twins Reared Apart: A Reanalysis*. New York: Basic Books).

41 See Shenk, 2011 (pp. 61–70). See note 40.
42 See Flynn, J. (1998) IQ gains over time: toward finding the causes, in U. Neisser (ed.) *The Rising Curve: Long-Term Gains in IQ and Related Measures*, pp. 25–66. Washington, DC: American Psychological Association.

Intelligence tests have to be recalibrated every few years to bring the mean score back to 100 (and to get girls equal with boys again as they keep pulling ahead). The significance of this was realized by James Flynn, who noticed the mean scores had always *risen* over the ten years or so between IQ test revisions. He calculated that there is a three-point improvement every decade, which means that someone who had an IQ of 100 and had been at the middle of the range in 1990 would have scored 115 in 1932 and been in the top 18 per cent. Flynn's own summary was that 'Data are now available for twenty nations and there is not a single exception to the findings of massive IQ gains over time' (p.26).

When he published these findings, Flynn was at a loss to explain them fully, especially as he did not believe common-sense intelligence had improved noticeably – we are not dramatically smarter than our grandparents in this respect. He subsequently came to an explanation that sits comfortably with the claims here about expertise, that the improvement over time was largely the result of *social multipliers*. He makes the point that scores on IQ subtests such as vocabulary, arithmetic and information have hardly changed, our grandparents needed these too, whereas the dramatic improvements have been on the more abstract subtests such as similarities and Raven's Matrices. This takes us back to Binet, intelligence can be improved and the 'brutal pessimism' of the hereditarians is misplaced, with the very groups they feared most, the poor and the minorities, gaining most.

See Flynn, J. (2006) Beyond the Flynn Effect: solution to all outstanding problems – except enhancing wisdom. Paper given at a presentation for The Psychometrics Centre, Cambridge Assessment. Cambridge: University of Cambridge.
43 Flynn, J. 1998 (p.3). See note 42.
44 Howe, 1999 (p.132). See note 12.
45 Shenk, 2011 (p.59). See note 40.
46 See more examples from Darold Treffert at https://www.wisconsinmedicalsociety.org/professional/savant-syndrome/savant-syndrome-overview [Accessed 31 July 2013].
47 Treffert, D. (2010) *Islands of Genius*, p.xv. London: Jessica Kingsley.

And here is another bizarre example. A 40-year-old dives into a shallow pool and suffers concussion. When he recovers he is able to play the piano and guitar – neither of which he could play pre-injury. He now composes film soundtracks and performs professionally.
48 Ibid.

49 Maguire, E.A., Gadian, D.G., Johnsrude, I.S., Good, C.D., Ashburner J., Frackowiak R.S.J. and Frith, C. (2000) Navigation-related structural change in the hippocampi of drivers, *Proceedings of the National Academy of Sciences*, 97(8): 4398–403.
50 Sternberg, 1999 (p.60). See note 24.
51 Howe, 1999 (p.15). See note 12.
52 Ceci, S.J. (1996) *On Intelligence: A Bioecological Treatise on Intellectual Development*. Cambridge, MA: Harvard University Press.
53 Gould, 1996. See note 39.
54 Sorokin, P. (1956) *Fads and Foibles of Modern Sociology and Related Sciences*. Chicago: Henry Regnery.
55 Feldman, H. (1984) A follow-up of subjects scoring above 180 IQ in Terman's genetic studies of genius, *Council for Exceptional Children*, 50(6): 518–23.
56 Woodhead, C. (2009) Don't say I was wrong, *Guardian*, 12 May. Available at http://www.guardian.co.uk/education/2009/may/chris-woodhead-teaching [Accessed 31 July 2013].

Chapter 2: How Experts Learn

57 See Colvin, G. (2008) *Talent Is Overrated: What Really Separates World-Class Performers from Everybody Else*. London: Nicholas Brealey.
58 Syed, 2010 (pp.63–70, 104). See note 5.
59 Ibid., p.104.
60 Gladwell, 2008 (pp.50–5). See note 4.
61 'Secondary modern' was the 1944 Education Act designation for the schools to which students who failed the 11+ went – some 70 per cent of the school population. They generally had low academic expectations and most students left without qualifications at the earliest opportunity. The shift to comprehensive schools in the 1970s improved expectations for many students, but in an area with selective schools the notion of 'secondary modern' lingered on.
62 Redgrave, S. (2009) *Inspired: Stories of Sporting Greatness*, p.277. London: Headline.
63 Ericsson et al., 1993 (pp.363–406). See note 8.
    An excellent overview of musical talent is found in John Slobada's chapter in Ericsson, K.A. (ed.) (2009) *The Road to Excellence: The Acquisition of Expert Performance in the Arts and Sciences, Sports, and Games*, pp.107–26. Hove: Psychology Press.
64 Smith, E. (2012) What some people call idleness is often the best investment. Available at http://www.newstatesman.com/business/business/2012/07/what-some-people-call-idleness-often-best-investment [Accessed 30 July 2012].

65 For those who need to know, it was the *layback Ina Bauer*.
66 Syed, 2010 (p.79). See note 5.
67 Barker, J. (2010) *The Brontës*, p.201. London: Abacus.
68 The term used by Anders Ericsson to capture memory skills, which can quickly recall items from long-term memory. Ericsson, K.A. and Kintsch, W. (1995) Long term working memory, *Psychological Review*, 102: 211–45.
69 Chi, 2006. See note 6.
70 Anderson, J.R. (1980) *Cognitive Psychology and Its Implications*, p.292. San Francisco: W.H. Freeman.
71 Endsley, M.R. (2006) Expertise and situation awareness, in Ericsson et al., 2006 (pp.633–51). See note 3.
72 Horswill, M.S., and Mckenna, F.P. (2004) Drivers' hazard perception ability: situation awareness on the road, in S. Banbury and S. Tremblay (eds), *A Cognitive Approach to Situation Awareness: Theory, Measurement and Application*, pp.155–75. Aldershot, UK: Ashgate Publishing.
73 Nietzsche, F. (1986) *Human, All Too Human: A Book for Free Spirits*: Cambridge: Cambridge University Press.

Chapter 3: Digging Deep: Expectations, Self-Belief and Challenge

74 Sherman, M. and Key, C.B. (1932) The intelligence of isolated mountain children, *Child Development*, 3(4): 279–90.
75 Csikszentmihalyi, M., Rathunde, K. and Whalen, S. (1997) *Talented Teenagers: The Roots of Success and Failure*. Cambridge: Cambridge University Press.
76 *Pride in Poor Maths 'Must Be Tackled'*. Available at http://www.bbc.co.uk/news/education-12525317 [Accessed 1 Jan. 2012].
77 Boaler, J. (2009) *The Elephant in the Classroom: Helping Children to Learn to Love Maths*, p.116. London: Souvenir Press.
78 Clark, L. (2010) Privately educated Michael Gove says 'rich, thick kids' do better than 'poor, clever children'. Available at http://www.dailymail.co.uk/news/article-1298425/Michael-Gove-says-rich-kids-better-poor-clever-children.html [Accessed 31 July 2013].
79 Hart, B. and Risley, T. (2003) The early catastrophe: the 30 million word gap by age 3, *American Educator*, 27: 1. Available at http://www.aft.org/newspubs/periodicals/ae/spring2003/hart.cfm [Accessed 31 July 2013].
80 The research evidence suggests it does for many teachers; see Brookhart, S. (2008) *How to Give Effective Feedback to Your Students*. Alexandria, VA: ASCD.

81 The full proficiency continuum moves through seven stages: naive, novice, initiate, apprentice, journeyman, expert and master (Chi, 2006. *See* note 6).

82 Driver, R., Squires, A., Rushworth, P. and Wood-Robinson, V. (1994) *Making Sense of Secondary Science: Research into Children's Ideas*. London: Routledge.

83 In Benjamin Bloom's classic study of exceptional children this was something that typically happened between 15 and 17 years of age. See Bloom, B (ed.) (1985) *Developing Talent in Young People*, pp.523–4. New York: Ballantine Books.

84 Feinstein, L. (2003) How early can we predict future educational achievement? Available at www.cep.lse.ac.uk/pubs/download/CP146.pdf [Accessed 31 July 2013]. The children in the sample were tested at 22 months and again at 3.5, 5 and 10 years and showed some different trajectories according to their social and economic status (SES). So 'social class stratification becomes more extreme by ten' (p.28). This is not all about the quality of schooling; the biggest relative gains and losses were between 22 and 42 months, but school is a factor.

85 Jerry, J. (2012) *The Socio-Economic Gradient in Teenagers' Literacy Skills: How Does England Compare to Other Countries?* DoQSS Working Paper No. 12–04, London: Institute of Education.

86 Reay, D. and Wiliam, D. (1999) 'I'll be a nothing': structure, agency and the construction of identity through assessment, *British Educational Research Journal*, 25: 343–54.

87 The eight-level system is intended as a progressive system in which pupils aged 7 are typically at level 2, and so by age 11 have moved to level 4. By age 14 they would typically be at levels 5–6.

88 *Times Educational Supplement*, p.13, Me level 4, you level 2 = end of friendship, 9 Feb. 2007.

89 Hattie, J. (2012) *Visible Learning for Teachers: Maximizing Impact on Learning*, p.30. London: Routledge.

90 The concepts of surface and deep learning were first developed by Marton, F. and Säljö, R. (1976) On qualitative differences in learning: 1 – outcome and process, *British Journal of Educational Psychology*, 46: 4–11.

91 Entwistle, N., McCune, V. and Walker, P. (2001) Conceptions, styles and approaches within higher education: analytic abstractions and everyday experience, in R. Sternberg and L. Zhang (eds) *Perspectives on Cognitive, Learning, and Thinking Styles*, pp.85–114. Mahwah, NJ: Lawrence Erlbaum. This approach has similarities to John West Burnham's *shallow, deep* and *profound* taxonomy. Available at http://www.johnwest-burnham.co.uk/index.php/understanding-deep-learning [Accessed 31 July 2013].

92 Louise Holden, There's no point in knowing about stuff that's not going to come up in exams, *Irish Times*, 27 Sept. 2005.

93 Ayres, P., Sawyer, W. and Dinham, S. (2004) Effective teaching in the context of a grade 12 high-stakes external examination in New South Wales, Australia, *British Educational Research Journal*, 30(1): 144–65 (both quotes on p.61).

94 Csikszentmihalyi, M. (1990) Literacy and intrinsic motivation, *Daedalus*, 19(2): 115–40 (p.118).

95 This section draws on Hidi and Harackiewicz, whose title this is. Hidi, S. and Harackiewicz, J.M. (2000) Motivating the academically unmotivated: a critical issue for the 21st century, *Review of Educational Research*, 70(2): 151–79.

96 Lumby, J. (2012) Disengaged and disaffected young people: surviving the system, *British Journal of Educational Research*, 38(2): 261–79 (p.270).

97 Stoll, L., Stobart, G., Martin, S. et al. (2003) *Preparing for Change: Evaluation of the Implementation of the Key Stage 3 Strategy Pilot*. London, DfES. See also Stobart, G. and Stoll, L. (2005) The Key Stage 3 strategy: what kind of reform is this? *Cambridge Journal of Education*, 35(2): 225–38.

98 Black, P., Harrison, C., Lee, C., Marshall, B. and Wiliam, D. (2003) *Assessment for Learning: Putting It into Practice*. Buckingham: Open University Press.

99 Pink, D. (2011) *Drive*, p.64. Edinburgh: Cannongate Books.

100 See Deci, E.L., Ryan, R.M. and Koestner, R. (1999) A meta-analysis review of experiments examining the effects of extrinsic rewards on intrinsic motivation, *Psychological Bulletin*, 125(6): 627–68.

101 Martin, A.J. (2006) Personal bests (PBs): a proposed multidimensional model and empirical analysis, *British Journal of Educational Psychology*, 76: 803–25 (p.804).

Chapter 4: Is Everybody Clear?

102 Harris, S., Wallace, G. and Rudduck, J. (1995) 'It's not that I haven't learnt much. It's just that I don't really understand what I'm doing': metacognition and secondary school students, *Research Papers in Education*, 10: 253–71.

103 Nater, S. and Gallimore, R. (2010) *You Haven't Taught Until They Have Learned*, p.10. Morgantown, WV: FIT.

104 Ibid., p.96.

105 Hattie, 2012 (p.17). See note 89.

106 Brookhart, S. (2010) *How to Assess Higher-Order Thinking Skills in Your Classroom*. Alexandria, VA: ASCD.

107 The Programme of International Student Achievement, the comparative testing of 15-year-olds that has become so important to governments as to where their country is in the international league table.

108 PISA http://www.oecd.org/edu/school/programmeforinternationalstudentas
sessmentpisa /33693997.pdf [Accessed 31 July 2013].

109 For a fuller treatment of this theme, see Stobart, 2008, Chapters 5–6. See note 27.

110 Gordon, S. and Reese, M. (1997) High stakes testing: worth the price? *Journal of School Leadership*, 7: 345–68 (p.364).

111 Eraut, M. (1997) Perspectives on defining 'the learning society', *Journal of Education Policy*, 12: 551–8 (p.556, his italics).

112 Knut Illeris in his authoritative *How We Learn* (Abingdon: Routledge, 2007) defines learning as 'any process that in living organisms leads to permanent capacity change and which is not solely due to biological maturation or ageing' (p.3).

113 Bloom, 1985. See note 83.

114 Biggs, J.B. and Collis, K.F. (1982) *Evaluating the Quality of Learning: The SOLO Taxonomy*. New York: Academic Press.

115 Biggs, J. and Tang, C. (2011) *Teaching for Quality Learning at University* (4th edn, p.100). Maidenhead: McGraw-Hill.

116 White, J. (ed.) (2004) *Rethinking the School Curriculum: The Next Stage in National Curriculum Reform*. London: RoutledgeFalmer.

117 Shulman, L.S. (1986) Those who understand: knowledge growth in teaching, *Educational Researcher*, 15(2): 4–14.

118 Hattie, 2012 (pp. 25–7). See note 89.

119 Heritage, M. (2011) Knowing what to do next: the hard part of formative assessment?, *CADMO*, 1: 67–84.

120 See Chapters 2–4 in Committee on How People Learn, A Targeted Report for Teachers, Center for Studies on Behavior and Development, National Research Council (2005) *How Students Learn: History, Mathematics, and Science in the Classroom*. Washington, DC: National Academies Press.

121 Brophy, J. (1998) Toward a model of the value aspect of motivation in education, pp. 5–6. Paper presented at American Educational Research Association, San Diego.

122 Hattie, 2012 (pp.51, 53). See note 89.

123 Petty, G. (2009) *Evidenced-Based Teaching* (2nd ed., pp.15–16). Cheltenham: Thomas Nelson.

124 From Boaler, 2009 (pp.38–9). See note 77.

And here are some solutions to compare with how you might have approached it:

1. 3 slices = $\frac{1}{3}$; x slices = $\frac{1}{4}$;
   cross-multiply so that $\frac{1}{3} x = \frac{1}{4}$,
   so $x = \frac{9}{4}$

2. If 3 slices is a third of a pound, then 9 slices is a pound. I can eat $\frac{1}{4}$ of a pound so $\frac{1}{4}$ of 9 slices is $\frac{9}{4}$ slices (Year 5)

Representing a pound: And then a quarter of a pound:

Figure 5 A visual solution

125 I prefer 'learning intentions' to 'learning objectives' because objectives, for me, have behaviourist associations with discrete tasks and very concrete learning. 'Intentions' have a more flexible and more general scope.
126 Adapted from Absolum, M. (2006) *Clarity in the Classroom*, p.85. Auckland, NZ: Hodder Education.
127 Gerver, R. (2010) *Creating Tomorrow's Schools Today*. London: Continuum.
128 Klein, G. (2011) *Streetlights and Shadows: Searching for the Keys to Adaptive Decision Making*, p.28. Cambridge, MA: MIT Press.
129 My thanks to Carol Evans for this example.
130 Hussey, T. and Smith, P. (2002) The trouble with learning outcomes, *Active Learning in Higher Education*, 3: 220–33 (pp. 230–2).
131 Torrance, H. (2005) *The Impact of Different Modes of Assessment on Achievement and Progress in the Learning and Skills Sector*, p.2. London: Learning and Skills Research Centre.
132 See his classic article: Sadler, D.R. (1989) Formative assessment and the design of instructional systems, *Instructional Science*, 18: 119–44.
133 From Gregory, K., Cameron, C. and Davies, A. (1997) *Setting and Using Criteria*, pp. 7–14. Melville, BC: Connections Publishing.
134 Brandt, R. (1993) On teaching for understanding: a conversation with Howard Gardner, *Educational Leadership*, 50(7): 4–7.
135 The long entry in Wikipedia shows the massive range of his interests and achievements: http://en.wikipedia.org/wiki/Benjamin_Franklin [Accessed 31 July 2013].
136 Colvin, 2008 (pp. 105–8). See note 57.

Chapter 5: Expert Diagnosis: the Teacher as Clinician

137 Ausubel, D. (1968) *Educational Psychology: A Cognitive View*, p.vi. New York: Holt, Rinehart and Winston.

138 Kassirer, J. (1995) Teaching problem-solving: how are we doing? *New England Journal of Medicine*, 332: 1507–9.

139 This section draws heavily on Patel, V.L., Kaufman, D.R. and Magder, S.A. (1996), The acquisition of medical expertise in complex dynamic environments, in Ericsson, 2009 (pp.127–65). *See* note 63. The fourth point is from Sanders, L. (2009) *Every Patient Tells a Story: Medical Mysteries and the Art of Diagnosis*. New York: Broadway Books. Lisa Sanders was the medical consultant for *House M.D.*

140 Ibid., p.6.

141 Alexander, R. (2004) *Towards Dialogic Teaching: Rethinking Classroom Talk*, pp.14–16. Cambridge: Dialogos.

142 Lumby, 2012 (p.269). See note 96.

143 I am indebted to the King's College London team, which includes Paul Black, Dylan Wiliam, Christine Harrison and Bethan Marshall, who have done much of the pioneering work in this area as well as Assessment for Learning in general. See their *Inside the Black Box* series (London: GL Assessment) for subject-specific examples.

   See Chapters 2–4 in Committee on How People Learn et al., 2005. *See* note 120.

144 Hattie, 2012. See note 89.

145 Other research puts the procedural as high as 30–60 per cent. However, the emphasis on factual recall has stayed much the same for over a century. A good summary is Steve Hastings (2012), Questioning, *Times Educational Supplement* magazine, 6 Oct. Available at http://www.tes.co.uk/article.aspx?storycode=381755 [Accessed 31 July 2013].

146 Motimore, P., Sammons, P., Stoll, L., Lewis, D. and Ecob, R. (1988), *School Matters: The Junior Years*. Somerset: Open Books.

147 Rowe, M.B. (1986) Wait time: slowing down may be a way of speeding up! *Journal of Teacher Education*, 1: 37–43.

148 *TES* Magazine (6 Oct. 2012) Questioning, tesconnect http://www.tes.co.uk/teaching-resource/Questioning-381755 [Accessed 4 Aug. 2013).

149 See Chapters 2–4 in Committee on How People Learn et al., 2005. See note 120.

150 Rowe, 1986. See note 147.

151 Black et al., 2003 (p.33). See note 98.

152 Pogrow, S. (2005) HOTS revisited: A thinking development approach to reducing the learning gap after grade 3, *Phi Delta Kappan*, 87(1): 64–75, quoted in Brookhart, 2010 (p.71). See note 106.

153 Feuerstein, R., Feuerstein, R.S., Falik, L. and Rand, Y. (2006) *Creating and Enhancing Cognitive Modifiability: The Feuerstein Instrumental Enrichment Program*, p.353. Jerusalem: ICELP Publications.

154 Ginsburg, H.P. (1997) *Entering the Child's Mind*, pp.14–15. Cambridge: Cambridge University Press.

155 Kress, G. (1999), A creative spell, *Guardian Education*, p.8, 26 Nov.

156 Sanders, 2009 (pp. 6–7). See note 139.

157 Postman, N. and Weingartner, C. (1971) *Teaching as a Subversive Activity*. London: Penguin Books.

158 This section draws on Mike Hughes's (2005) excellent *Lessons Are for Learning*, pp. 31–40. Stafford: Network Educational Press.

159 This is an approach used in highly effective maths lessons in Japan. The teacher sets a problem (without teaching) and groups try to solve it. If they do, they are then encouraged to set problems for the other groups. See Stigler, J.W. and Hiebert, J. (1999) *The Teaching Gap: Best Ideas from the World's Teachers for Improving Education in the Classroom*, New York: Free Press.

160 Black et al., 2003 (p.5). See note 98.

161 Sanders, 2009. See note 139.

Chapter 6: Getting and Giving Feedback: It's Harder Than We Think

162 Kluger, A. and DeNisi, A. (1996) The effects of feedback interventions on performance: a historical review, a meta-analysis and a preliminary feedback intervention theory, *Psychological Bulletin*, 119(2): 254–84 (p.274).

163 Wiliam, D. (2011) *Embedded Formative Assessment*, p.127. Bloomington: Solution Tree Press – an excellent source of practical classroom ideas.

164 The researchers were Ron Gallimore and Roland Tharp, who adapted their findings into the award-winning KEEP programme of reading development (Wooden himself was an ex-English teacher). Their book based on this was *Rousing Minds to Life: Teaching, Learning and Schooling in a Social Context*. New York: Cambridge University Press. See also Coyle, 2010 (pp.167–72). See note 15.

165 Tescoverstory, 'I wouldn't be where I am today', *Times Educational Supplement*, p.24, 29 Apr. 2013.

166 And the Nobel Prize goes to . . . the man ridiculed at school for science ambitions, *Guardian*, p.3, 9 Oct. 2012.

167 See Dweck, C. (2000) *Self-Theories*, pp.117–19. Hove: Psychology Press. This is an excellent book on how students think about their ability to learn – and how 'fixed ability' thinking gets in the way.

168 Gawande, A. (2003) *Complications: A Surgeon's Notes on an Imperfect Science*, p.58. London: Profile Books.

169 James, M., McCormick, R., Black, P. et al. (2007) *Improving Learning How to Learn: Classrooms, Schools and Networks*. TLRP Improving Learning Series, London: Routledge. See Chapter 3. Bethan Marshall, Patrick Carmichael and Mary-Jane Drummond make the distinction between the 'spirit' and 'letter' of

assessment for learning. This for me has somewhat religious overtones ('do
you have the spirit?'). I prefer the more neutral distinction between 'routine
expertise' (doing what's in the manual) and 'adaptive expertise' in which an
understanding of the principles allows a far more flexible approach.
170 Carless, D. (2007) 'conceptualising pre-emptive formative assessment',
Assessment in Education: Principles, Policy and Practice, 14(2): 171–84.
171 For a fuller account, see Stigler and Hiebert, 1999. See note 159.
172 See http://lessonstudy.co.uk/about-us-pete-dudley [Accessed 24 Apr. 2013].
173 Hattie, J. and Timperley, H. (2007) The power of feedback, *Review of
Educational Research*, 77: 81–112 (p.104).
174 Kluger and DeNisi, 1996. See note 162. For a more readable account
see Hattie and Timperley, 2007. See note 173. See also Valerie Shute's
(2007) *Focus on Formative Feedback*, ETS Research Reports, Princeton,
NJ: Educational Testing Service. Available at http://www.ets.org/research/
researcher/RR-07-11.html [Accessed 31 July 2013].
175 Clarke, S. (2003) *Enriching Feedback in the Primary Classroom*. London:
Hodder and Stoughton.
176 Csikszentmihalyi et al., 1997 (p.14, my italics). See note 75.
177 Personal communication. See Johnston, P.H. (2004) *Choice Words: How Our
Language Affects Children's Learning*. Portland: Stenhouse Publishers.
178 Dweck, 2000, Chapter 16. See note 167.
179 This comes from Kluger and DeNisi's complex theorizing of how feedback
works. Kluger and DeNisi, 1996. *See* note 162.
180 He outlines prompt levels 1–3. Absolum, 2006 (pp.122–5). See note 126.
181 This is Eleanore Hargreaves's very useful concept.
182 Brookhart, 2008 (pp.109–10). See note 80.
183 The classic evidence is the work of Ruth Butler: Butler, R. (1988) Enhancing
and undermining intrinsic motivation: the effect of task-involving and ego-
involving evaluation on interest and performance, *British Journal of Educational
Psychology*, 58: 1–14.
    I find Lipnevich and Smith's prize-winning research on praise and marks
with first-year university students even more convincing: Lipnevich, A. and
Smith, J. (2009) Effects of differential feedback on students' examination
performance, *Journal of Experimental Psychology: Applied*, 15: 319–33.
    Alfie Kohn is a powerful arguer against current grading practices because
of the way they affect learning. See http://www.alfiekohn.org/ [Accessed 31
July 2013].
184 Csikszentmihalyi et al., 1997 (p.182). See note 75.
185 Thanks here to my hosts Anne Jacobsen and Geir Willard.
186 Petty, 2009 (p.92). See note 123.
187 Wiliam, 2011 (p.131). See note 163.
188 Petty, 2009 (p.90). See note 123.

189 Clarke, S. (2001) *Unlocking Formative Assessment*. London: Hodder and Stoughton.
190 Hattie, 2012 (p.121). See note 89.
191 See ibid., pp.120–1, for a good summary and further references. Alfie Kohn's *Punished by Rewards: The Trouble with Gold Stars, Incentive Plans, A's, Praise, and Other Bribes* (Boston: Houghton Mifflin, 1999) is, as you might gather from the title, a spirited attack on much that claims to be feedback.
192 Petty, 2009 (pp.260–1). See note 123.

Chapter 7: The Expert School

193 Quoted in Klein, G. (2011) *Streetlights and Shadows: Searching for the Keys to Adaptive Decision Making*, p.110. Cambridge, MA: MIT Press.
194 Ibid., pp.310–11.
195 Gunzenhauser, M. (2003) High-stakes testing and the default philosophy of education, *Theory into Practice*, 42: 51–8 (p.51).
196 Ibid.
197 James et al., 2007. See note 169.
198 Fullan, M. and Hargreaves, A. (1996) *What's Worth Fighting for in Your School*. New York: Teachers College Press. This has been updated as Hargreaves, A. and Fullan, M. (2012) *Professional Capital: Transforming Teaching in Every School*. London: Routledge. See also Stoll, L., Fink, D. and Earl, L. (2003) *It's About Learning (and It's About Time): What's in It for Schools?*, London: RoutledgeFalmer.
199 Syed, 2010 (p.51). *See* note 5.
200 See   http://en.wikipedia.org/w/index.php?title=Laura_Trott&oldid=564380316 [Accessed 31 July 2013].
201 Coyle, 2010 (p.59). *See* note 15. I draw on his account of the Z-Boys. His broader argument is that practice lays down myelin sheathing in the nervous system, so the more pathways are used, the faster the transmission. So skill is 'insulation that wraps neural circuits and grows according to certain signals' (p.73). For those interested in the biology of skill development his book makes a provocative case.
202 A first-hand account appears in Syed 2010 (pp.27–35). See note 5.
203 Ibid., p.32.
204 These can be accessed through the *Times Educational Supplement* website http://www.tes.co.uk/article.aspx?storycode [Accessed 31 July 3013].
205 'ESN' is Educationally Sub-Normal, now replaced with the less emotive Special Educational Needs (SEN).

206 Ordinary (O) levels, taken at 16, were intended for the top 20 per cent of students. Advanced (A) levels were even more selective and geared to university admission. O levels were largely replaced in England by the General Certificate of Secondary Education (GCSE), which is taken by over 80 per cent of students.

207 Pink, 2011 (p.64). See note 99.

208 Bloom, 1985. See note 83. Csikszentmihalyi et al., 1997. See note 75.

209 Stigler and Hiebert, 1999. See note 159.

210 For example, Pelligrino, J.W., Chowdowsky, N. and Glaser, R. (2001) *Knowing What Students Know: The Science and Design of Educational Assessment.* Washington, DC: National Academy Press.
    For student responses, see Lumby, 2012. See note 96. Stoll et al., 2003. See note 97.

211 Two starters here are Mercer, N. (2000) *Words and Minds: How We Use Language to Think Together.* London: Routledge and Mercer, N. and Littleton, K. (2007) *Dialogue and the Development of Children's Thinking: A Sociocultural Approach.* London: Routledge. A summary by Neil Mercer can be found at http://www.youtube.com/watch?v=nK9-qMDGITo [Accessed 31 July 2013].

212 Sir Peter Lampl's *Sutton Trust*, which campaigns for better opportunities for state-educated children, is a constant source of valuable data about the inequalities of educational opportunities in the UK. See, for example, *The Educational Backgrounds of Leading Lawyers, Journalists, Vice Chancellors, Politicians, Medics and Chief Executives.* The Sutton Trust submission to the Milburn Commission on access to the professions, March 2009.

213 BBC *News*, 3 Aug. 2012. Available at http://www.bbc.co.uk/news/education-19109724 [Accessed 2 Feb. 2013].

214 Vygotsky, L. (1978) *Mind in Society: The Development of Higher Psychological Processes.* Cambridge, MA: Harvard University Press (ebook version).

215 Hargreaves and Fullan, 2012 (p.46). See note 198.

216 Stigler and Hiebert, 1999 (p.134). See note 159.

217 See Richard Wagner and Keith Stanovitich's Expertise in reading, in Ericsson, 2009 (Chapter 7). See note 63.

218 See pp. 59–60 in Adams, M.J. (1990) *Beginning to Read: Thinking and Learning About Print.* Cambridge, MA: MIT Press.

219 Boaler, 2009 (p.103). See note 77.

220 Dewey, J. (1933) *How We Think* (p.236). Lexington, MA: Heath.

221 Bloom, 1985 (p.413). See note 83.

222 Csikszentmihalyi et al., 1997 (p.219). See note 75.

223 Ericsson, 2009 (pp.21–2). See note 63.

224 Brandt, 1993. See note 134.

225 Holt, 1982 (pp.274–5). See note 2.

226 *The Sunday Times*, p.15, 5 Feb. 2012, Oh well done class, you are all total flops.
227 Hargreaves and Fullan, 2012. See note 198.
228 Dewey, 1933 (pp.78–9). See note 220.

Select Bibliography

General reading on expertise and ability

Colvin, G. (2008) *Talent Is Overrated: What Really Separates World-Class Performers from Everybody Else*. London: Nicholas Brealey. A highly readable account geared to a business audience.

Gladwell, M. (2008) *Outliers: The Story of Success*. London: Allen Lane. A provocative bestseller – highly readable and a good starting place.

Shenk, D. (2011) *The Genius in All of Us: Why Everything You've Been Told about Genetics, Talent and Intelligence Is Wrong*. London: Icon Books. Despite its abrasive title, this is a remarkably erudite book, particularly on genetics.

Syed, M. (2010) *Bounce: How Champions Are Made*. London: Fourth Estate. A well-researched and well-written bestseller by a former champion and current *Times* sports writer.

Directly related to teaching and learning

Absolum, M. (2006) *Clarity in the Classroom*. Auckland, NZ: Hodder Education. A valuable practical guide to learning intentions, and more, which draws on experience from New Zealand.

Boaler, J. (2009) *The Elephant in the Classroom: Helping Children to Learn to Love Maths*. London: Souvenir Press. A passionate account of how to raise expectations and outcomes for all students in mathematics.

Brookhart, S. (2008) *How to Give Effective Feedback to Your Students*. Alexandria, VA: ASCD. Geared to American education, this is a good source of practical ideas on how to give effective feedback.

Hattie, J. (2012) *Visible Learning for Teachers: Maximizing Impact on Learning*. London: Routledge. An invaluable source of international evidence about what practices work (and what don't) to improve learning and teaching.

Hughes, M. (2005) *Lessons Are for Learning*. Stafford: Network Educational Press. This imaginative book encourages deeper learning by providing ideas and practices for teachers.

Petty, G. (2009) *Evidenced-Based Teaching* (2nd edn). Cheltenham: Thomas Nelson. This edition takes John Hattie's findings and provides a wealth of examples of how to turn them into practical teaching strategies.

Swann, M., Peacock, A., Hart, S. and Drummond M.J. (2012) *Creating Learning Without Limits*. Maidenhead: Open University Press. A case study of a primary school challenging fixed ability thinking and seeking to provide opportunities for all students.

Wiliam, D. (2011) *Embedded Formative Assessment*. Bloomington: Solution Tree Press. Though Dylan Wiliam has written this primarily for American educators, it is directly relevant to teachers in other cultures through the many ideas and examples it provides.

Index

185

Wiltshire, Stephen 32
Wooden, John 81–2, 90, 95, 123, 134
Woodhead, Chris 35–6
Woods, Tiger 13, 28, 45
Wragg, Ted 111
Wrong answers 108, 115–18

Z
Z-Boys 145
Zones 51–3, 88, 105
   comfort 3, 49, 50–3, 55, 88, 105, 151, 153, 159
   learning 51–2, 55, 88, 105, 138, 160
   Panic 51–2, 88, 105, 128

BAD EDUCATION
Debunking Myths in Education

Philip Adey and Justin Dillon (Eds)

9780335246014 (Paperback)
2012

eBook also available

We all know that small classes are better than large classes; that children are best taught in groups according to their ability; that some schools are much better than others and that we should teach children according to their individual learning styles ... or do we?

This book asks awkward questions about these and many other sacred cows of education. Each chapter tackles a persistent myth in education, confronting it with research evidence and teasing out any kernel of truth which may underlie the myth.

Key features:

- The 17 chapters each deal with one topic and are written by an established authority in the field
- The arguments are defensible and underpinned by sound
- Covers topical issues such as the class size debate – *Class Size: Is Small Better?* and the question *Are there "Good" and "Bad" Schools?*

www.openup.co.uk